Back of the Shaft

Memories of a Life in Murton
in the 1950s

by P.J. McPartland

A postcard view of Murton Railway Station.

Summerhill Books

Summerhill Books publishes local history books on Durham, Northumberland and Tyneside. To receive a catalogue of our titles send a stamped addressed envelope to:

Andrew Clark, Summerhill Books, PO Box 1210, Newcastle-upon-Tyne NE99 4AH

or email: summerhillbooks@yahoo.co.uk

or visit our website to view our full range of books:
www.summerhillbooks.co.uk

Copyright P.J. McPartland 2013

First published in 2013 by

Summerhill Books
PO Box 1210, Newcastle-upon-Tyne NE99 4AH

www.summerhillbooks.co.uk

email: summerhillbooks@yahoo.co.uk

ISBN: 978-1-906721-66-4

Contents

The old Murton Police Station that looked down the Terrace.

Introduction

A few years ago, I wrote an illustrated memoir of a childhood spent in the pit village of Murton during the 1940s. I called it Pit Boy. The reception accorded the book was encouraging and, since then, I often thought of writing a sequel celebrating the 1950s. However, for a long time I remained doubtful that I would find enough to write about. Finally, I sat down and drafted a first chapter, then a second, then more chapters as one by one the memories came springing to my mind. Back of the Shaft is the result.

As in Pit Boy, it became necessary sometimes to use fictitious names. This applies mainly to people who appear only briefly in the book, and whose real names after so long an interval of time are impossible to recall. Places like Cornwall, Fatten Pasture, the Terrace and the Cornfield, are mentioned only in passing as they were described in full in the first book.

I fancy many will think me an incurable sentimentalist, something I have no wish to deny. Past associations are precious to me. The original volume, Pit Boy, contained a dedication to my grandchildren. I take pleasure in dedicating the present volume, Back of the Shaft, to all Murtonians living and dead.

P.J. McPartland

An illustration of the path through Murton Dene, above Dalton-le-Dale.

Chapter One
The Lie of the Land

Durham is a very hilly county; and in that respect Murton is the County in miniature. Almost wherever you live in Murton you will live on a hill or at the foot of a hill; and Murton's schools, churches, shops and public buildings nearly all stand, or once stood, in this relation.

Three roads run through Murton, excluding those that wander around the housing estates. They rise, often imperceptibly, at times steeply, in an east-west direction. The main road, the B1285, branches from the Sunderland to Stockton road at Cold Hesledon, in former times the scene of a flourishing community, since supplanted by industrial units. Flanked on one side by the Dalton Park Retail Centre, the B1285 enters Murton at a point once commanded by the signal box on a mineral railway crossing. Beyond, lay the grey frontage of Murton Street and the broad expanse of the colliery marshalling yard.

Across the way, several rows of colliery houses had at one time run off at right angles to the main road; demolished more than seventy years ago, the area is now grassed over.

Murton Street as it looked in the 1950s has long gone, and the once lacklustre prospect of rough-and-ready 19th century

Murton Street before the Second World War.

housing has been superseded by the more sanitized outlook afforded by new apartment blocks, private, detached dwellings, and, in a further nod to modernity, the multi-purpose, state-of-the-art Glebe Centre.

Only yards from the Glebe Centre stands an abandoned pub. The pub sign once proclaimed it to be the Traveller's Rest, an apt designation seeing as it was the first hostelry the traveller would happen upon on entering Murton. But only strangers ever dignified it thus. To locals it was invariably known as the Back of the Shaft. The pub holds a special place in my remembrance, calling to mind a disreputable episode in the past. For it was in the Back of the Shaft in the mid 1950s that I became an under age drinker and indulged a rapidly acquired taste for Scotch beer.

Cookson Terrace on the corner opposite runs parallel to the B1285, ending at a cultivated plot of land where a house once stood. According to Helen Abbott, the author of the history of Murton up to the 1960s, the house had been built for Murton's first

The Travellers Rest or Back of the Shaft. Today it is renamed and boarded for sale.

The old Travellers Rest with its 'select room' on the right.

schoolmaster. Subsequently, it became the original premises of the Murton branch of the Co-op, before the move to Woods Terrace. In the 1940s, it was a fish and chip shop, and the building had a chequered history ever since then. When it stood derelict a few years ago, I wrote a letter to the Sunderland Echo complaining that it should have been allowed to fall into such a state of disrepair. Citing Mrs Abbott, I recalled the building's background and antiquity, in the sure belief that my advocacy would prompt the authorities into taking the necessary action. I awaited the start of renovation work. I imagined how the old building would look when restored to its original condition, with possibly a small ceremony to mark its

A postcard for Murton Colliery Co-operative Society.

reopening. I thought of my timely intercession and swelled with pride. Two weeks later, the building was razed to the ground. It is possible, I suppose, that the building was in such a dilapidated state it was beyond saving, and that my letter of complaint had forced the authorities' hand. But I hate to think that, however well-intentioned, and albeit indirectly, it was I who had administered the coup de grace.

CHURCH ST. and MINERS' HALL, MURTON COLLIERY. 1638.

Church Street with the Colliery Inn and Miners' Hall further on.

The stretch of road known as Church Street used to be fronted by terraced cottages of a type seen in many pit villages of the North East. They were built of local stone, in colour a washed out yellow, uniformly cut into square blocks. Elegance was sacrificed to utility as the coal owners and the pace of the industry required that the dwellings be constructed with the utmost haste. Still, once the threshold had been crossed they could be very homely, as I can personally testify. Those past the junction of Church Street and Coronation Street South had at some time been bulldozed, and the land was not reused until the 1960s, when South View came into existence. During the war, a water tank occupied the site, the bottom of which was always littered with half bricks. The housing after South View is mostly turn of the century. Brunini's ice cream parlour was situated in the middle of Victoria Terrace, and was at one time a popular Sunday afternoon rendezvous for the young. Facing Brunini's, roughly between the Victoria Club and the Victoria Inn or "High House", a solid brick edifice with a sheer pitched roof overshadowed the road. The ground floor comprised a sweet shop and the living accommodation was above the shop. Mr and Mrs Shaw, the elderly couple who ran the shop, never seemed to be swamped with customers. Their busiest time was when they were serving people who were on their way to the nearby Olympia picture house. Brunini's later became a grocer's shop; Shaw's shop and the building it

The Victoria Inn or 'High House'.

7

occupied disappeared some years ago, a fate that also befell the Olympia, which was demolished to make way for private housing.

Looming into view past the end of Victoria Terrace, the Democratic Club made more of a visual impact than its older rival, the Victoria or "Big Club", which in appearance was and is fairly unassuming. You had to walk up to the Demi. It was accessed by a courtyard, and a stately flight of steps flanked by metal banisters, well polished by the seat of many a pair of boys' trousers. A serious fire at one time resulted in the club being gutted and almost completely rebuilt. At the time of writing, the Big Club is still extant. Sadly, after being closed and having at least one attempt to reopen it come to nought, the Demi was finally pulled down. Its place has been taken by an aged people's home.

From the home, the road ascends at a barely discernible increase to St Joseph's churchyard. The church itself is a striking example of 1960s church building and completely dominates the road at this point. Its predecessor, the old tin church, was throughout its lifetime surrounded by trees, which obliterated from view all but the roof of the church. There now commences one of those steep inclines that typify Murton, before the road arrives at the gates of the parish church of Holy Trinity, atop of the aptly named church bank. Across the road, a tarmac path slopes off past the periphery of Murton Cemetery to the Murton Welfare Park, a half mile below. There is some very pleasing private housing on the south side, which gazes out beyond the cemetery and the park in the direction of neighbouring South Hetton. From Vicarage Terrace, so named for the old vicarage close by, the B1285 maintains a steady upward progress, until, after three or four hundred yards, it climbs to another summit, emerging at the Cenotaph in the heart of Murton Village.

Commemorating the Murton men who lost their lives in the Great War, to which were later added the names of the war dead of the Second World War, Murton Cenotaph is a most imposing example of the kind, believed to be modelled on the Cenotaph in Whitehall. The place used sometimes to be called the Village Park. Then it was fenced all round

Two views of Murton Cenotaph.

with entrance gates on two sides and park benches in various parts. It made for a restful mood. Old men were drawn to the seated pavilion inside the boundary fence, here to pass the time of day, in contemplation perhaps, while enjoying a quiet smoke. An irregular patch of green west of the Cenotaph is the nearest Murton has to a village green. On the margin, consonant with the rustic symmetry of neighbouring farmhouse and converted barn, stands that other facet of the English rural scene, the village pub. Murton Village is

a mix of private habitation, old and new, and ancient farm buildings. Although building works have gone on to the north and south, the village itself still manages to present a rural atmosphere and charm.

Past the Village Inn and Raine's farm right of the road, progress is fairly even. Then, for the last quarter of a mile, the B1285 gradually falls away before leaving Murton where once a passenger railway crossing and signal box marked the point of departure. The Store bakery once flourished a short distance west of here; the hall adjacent to it provided the venue where members of the Amateur Operatic Society met to rehearse. A single row of bungalows skirting the road right of the crossing is the last sign of human habitation. The road now goes into a dip before entering upon its longest and steepest course, taking it to the top of Murton Moor Farm, after which a rambling route across open country brings it to the neighbouring pit village of Hetton-le-Hole.

The greater part of Murton is out of sight of the B1285. Yet for two miles, from one rail crossing to the next, the road passed by all but one of Murton's pubs, two working men's clubs, several places of worship and a school; and two of Murton's three cinemas were only yards away. While some of these institutions have met with closure, most still remain.

A second road begins as a footpath through the dene above Dalton-le-Dale and is interrupted by the A19. The footpath becomes a road when it emerges from the dene at a spot where formerly Dene Terrace ended, about a hundred yards from the colliery manager's house. From here, the road bisects a wide expanse of open ground. Dene Terrace, Salisbury Place and the farmhouse and tied cottages of Fatten Pasture have all disappeared, and much of the land is grassed over. The old allotments survive as a relic of former times. I knew them as an infant; although allotments look the same the world over.

The colliery dwellings of Cornwall were demolished in the late 1950s and the area transformed by what was then modern housing. Today, on the opposite side of the road, horses rove over a pastoral landscape. One of the great coal-producing pits of the Industrial Revolution fell silent in 1991, and land which had been the scene of heavy industry for a century and a half has reverted to pasture.

A lone horse on the former site of Murton Colliery. A rural scene has now replaced what was once a thriving industrial landscape.

Half a mile from its beginning, possibly more, the road arrives at the edge of what, with a little imagination, could be called the town centre. Here the road is at its widest point, presided over, on the one side, by the Independent Methodist Church and an ex-servicemen's club, formerly the Temperance Institute, and, on the other side, by a building that was originally the Murton Police Station. Now the road rises steeply for about two hundred yards, before levelling off past the library at the junction of Barnes Road and Toft Crescent.

Countless numbers of Murton children passed through the Council School, which, until recently, stood opposite the library. Alas, it is gone, and the shrill sound of youthful voices that once regularly filled the air is heard no more. The school's days were numbered when schoolchildren began to be bussed out of the community to comprehensives in other parts of the County. After serving the community of Murton for almost a century, the school was closed and soon after levelled.

Barnes Road, as this stretch of the road is known, is comprised mostly of retired people's bungalows maintained by the local authority. Over to the right hand side, beyond the irregular contours of what remains of the Cornfield and the perimeter housing of Burnip Road, a broad, rustic panorama meets the eye. At the centre point of field and woodland, some three miles distant, the ancient settlement of Warden Law may just be glimpsed. Previously it was unmissable, but years of quarrying have reduced the once imperial Warden

EAST MURTON. 1637.

Two postcard views of Murton Village.

Law Hill to no more than a ragged protuberance on the horizon. It was at Warden Law that the monks of Lindisfarne paused to rest during their odyssey to seek a home for the body of St. Cuthbert. They found one at Chester-le-Street, before eventually removing to Durham, where the cathedral was built as the saint's final resting place.

After a few hundred yards on the flat, the road comes up to the landmark building of Murton Hostel. Originally an abode for homeless men, it ceased to serve this purpose some time ago, when it was converted into flats. From the Hostel, the road rears upwards, curving past the Aged Miners' Homes until it merges with the B1285 at the Cenotaph.

Once a bustling commercial thoroughfare, Murton Terrace takes its departure from the B1285 at the Colliery Inn. Although the bottom end has become somewhat run down, the Terrace retains a tolerable aspect at the centre. A road deviates from it at the Store Clock and proceeds along Western Terrace to the single major crossroads in Murton. Here, it is bisected by the only road of significance, apart from the Terrace, running in a north-south direction, one that connects with all of Murton's three arterial roads.

The Colliery Inn – in 2013 this pub stands closed like many local pubs.

The shop on the corner of Coronation Street West was Glassford's sweet shop in the fifties. It was said of it then that it was the only three storey house in Murton. If true, it no longer enjoys that reputation. The Church Huts at the foot of the Inventor streets opposite was the venue for many dances and celebrations. It was spacious, with a good floor for dancing. The Church Huts disappeared some years ago. There is only one phase of the present road where it marks an ascent; that is where it leaves the crossroads and climbs to the former site of the Rex cinema. The Rex once crowned the pinnacle of two hills; or possibly it was two sides of the same hill. As the Council Schools once dominated the skyline to the north and north-east, so the Rex, together with Holy Trinity Church, reigned over the south side of Murton to the margin of South Hetton.

Passing the end of the terraced streets of Harrogate and Ripon, the road progresses along Williams Road, skirting Holy Trinity churchyard opposite, until it arrives at the former Knaresborough public house at the junction of Porter Terrace. Built in the early 1930s on the edge of a new council housing estate, the Knaresborough recently suffered closure, but has now reopened as a private dwelling. There is little else of note here, and barely two hundred yards past the Knaresborough the road joins the B1285 just below Murton Village.

Throughout its history as a pit village, Murton experienced many changes; as a former pit village it is continually changing. My paternal grandparents both died in the early 1920s, and so knew nothing of the vast extent of council house building that went on before and after the Second World War. Their world was confined to the east of

Murton, in close proximity to the pit. Beyond that, lay rolling fields. They, and Murtonians long dead, I suspect would be staggered to find the Murton of their day transformed beyond their imagining. But not entirely beyond their recognition, I think. For certain things endure unchanged. Familiar landmarks such as Holy Trinity Church and Batter Law Hill remain constant. And the lie of the land changes very little if at all.

A rural scene south-west of Murton.

Chapter Two
On the Belts

Barring chronic ill health, you could always find a job at the pit. Occasionally, a lad might leave school unable to read, giving rise to fears concerning his ability to comprehend danger signs. However, a job of some description could usually be found. So long as the pit remained operational, virtually no able bodied man in Murton was unemployable.

I left school at fifteen with no qualifications and no prospects beyond a job for life at Murton Colliery. It was early 1952, a few years after nationalization, and coal production was at a peak. Coal miners were exempted from National Service so great was the demand for coal. The industrial unrest of a generation or so earlier, while it might have left bitter memories, was a thing of the past. There had been no strikes since the General Strike of 1926. With full employment went an improvement in living standards; and, thanks to the sweeping social reforms of the post war Labour government, there was a preponderate sense of security.

After a medical and an interview with the Safety Officer and various other required procedures, I was passed fit for work on the belts, which was the usual apprenticeship for boys destined to work underground. The procedure at the Pit Head Baths was the first thing I had to get used to. The baths marked a relatively recent advancement in working conditions. In his volume on County Durham in The Buildings of England series, the renowned authority on British architecture, Nicholas Pevsner, praised Murton Pit Head Baths as a building of note. It was the only building in Murton to receive the accolade.

There were two levels to the baths, upper and lower levels being identical in layout and purpose. Every man had a clean locker and a dirty locker. Before the shift began, you got out of your clean, everyday clothes, carefully hanging them in the clean locker. Then, draped in a bath towel, and with bare feet thrust uncomfortably inside your shoes, you shuffled along to the corresponding row of lockers on the other side of the building. After donning pit clothes from the dirty locker and swapping shoes for hob nailed pit boots, towel, soap and flannel were put away and the key turned in the lock.

Murton Colliery provided work for many local men.

The procedure was reversed on completion of the shift. The dusty work clothes were first hung up and locked away; then, after a hot shower, you would slip into the clothes that you had left in the clean locker.

Not two hundred yards from the relative calm of the baths, amid the tumult at bank, men toiled all day long effortlessly moving coal tubs about. Tubs propelled from the pit cage full (fullens), were in a short while conveyed empty (chummins) to another cage and another pit shaft for the return journey to the coal face. At certain times of the day, these operations were suspended, and men rode the twin deck cage, their shift over, or not yet begun. But at bank, the hours were mostly occupied by men engaged in the business of shifting coal. Once a coal tub had left the cage, it was weighed, and then manoeuvred onto a turntable which rotated the tub a full 360 degrees, causing it to disgorge its contents into a hopper. The coals were then sieved of small stuff; at the same time they were shaken down to a moveable belt. The belt ran from end to end of a long shed, before off-loading the coals into a wagon below.

Concessionary coals were delivered to the door of the house unscreened; but saleable coal had first to be picked clean of stones. Boys hunched over the moving belt at intervals of a few feet, singling out stones from among the coal, before casting them down chutes and into wagons stationed outside. Overall, from the arrival of coals at

Murton Colliery's pit head baths.

bank to the selection process at the belts, it was a system of great efficiency which ran generally without hindrance or interruption.

Most of my workmates on the belts were, like me, new to the work. One or two, like Jim Laws, were by now old hands, having left school a term earlier than the rest of us. Five of the new starters travelled the few miles from another colliery village, where they had been unable to obtain places on the belts of their local pit. They stuck together to begin with, drawing comfort from a shared familiarity, but soon mixed in with the rest of us. The irrepressible Baxter Malbete soon became a close friend of mine. In no time at all, a bond of comradeship developed from which no one was excluded. Altogether, a more congenial crew of fresh-faced neophytes never worked the belts.

We worked under the supervision of an adult foreman or keeker, each man at his station, hands employed in quick, flailing movements, separating stones from coal as the belt passed by. The stones came in varying sizes; huge slabs had to be picked up in both hands and heaved beyond the belt and onto the chute. Often they got stuck at the neck of the chute and had to be broken up with the aid of a pinch bar. It then became necessary to lean over the belt in order to stab at the obstruction, a task which was made awkward by the weight of the pinch bar and the constantly moving belt. The furthest man on the belt was seldom overworked, as most of the screening had been done by the time the belt passed him by. But every now and then if there was an excessive amount of stone present, he would shift along to the end with a quick, side-stepping motion to dispose of the remaining stones before the contents of the belt could empty into the wagon below. I worked alongside Baxter, who was always cheerful, and an occasional source of amusement to the rest of us. It was soon noticed that he almost always had banana sandwiches for his bait; and even if he had something else in his sandwiches, his bait would include a banana. We began calling him the Banana Kid, which, in a very short while, was abbreviated to Kiddo.

Men working on the belts in two Durham collieries.

The overriding impression of the belts, at once the most palpable and inescapable impression, was the noise. You were made aware of it while still well out of sight of the place; an interminable din of squealing machinery of a level so loud it made normal conversation impossible. There was no relief from it, for only rarely was the belt brought to a standstill. To communicate with your nearest neighbour, who could be only three feet away, it was necessary to shout at the highest pitch of

your voice. A system of hand signals had long ago been devised for contact with those further down the line. Mostly the system was confined to requests from those wishing to know the time of day. A circular motion of the hand before the face signified the hour; a hand at the throat and two fingers raised a quarter to the hour; a sweeping gesture of the arm away from the waist half past the hour and so on. Yet even though we were hardly able to hear our own voices, in the age-old tradition of labouring folk, we sang. Catchy, currently popular songs, such as Shrimp Boats and Hey Round the Corner, helped us keep our spirits up. At least you could hear the tune in your mind.

But more onerous even than the noise, which you could almost get used to, was the sheer drudgery of performing mechanical tasks for hours on end in a stationary position. There

Jo Stafford who recorded 'Shrimp Boats' – one of the songs we sang on the belts.

14

could be no getting used to the spirit-numbing boredom that made the hours drag by. The fitters and blacksmiths in the workshops worked shorter hours than we did. Every day, we listened for the sound of the hooter, faintly echoing above the squealing of the belt, that told us that they had finished work for the day. Then we knew we had only two hours to go before our shift was up; before lowse, as was the common expression.

The keekers worked in rotation, so one week we would have Jack Mustard supervising and the next week it would be Ernie Ridley. Both were friendly, if taciturn, men. When Ernie was in charge, he would let one or other of us knock off work when there was about twenty minutes of the shift still remaining. Everyone got his turn. Ernie would come and clap a hand on somebody's shoulder and incline his head in the direction of the iron stairway. Without a backward glance, the lucky individual would quickly scamper up the stairway and disappear. He would be showered and changed and most likely on his way home before the rest of us had been loused out.

On rare occasions of fleeting duration when coals failed to arrive on the belt, it was possible to enjoy a few minutes respite in the bait cabin at the top of the stairs. The bait cabin was solely for our use, the keekers having their own sanctum. Brick built, with a corrugated iron roof and wooden seating within, it was a cosy little retreat, if only we had sufficient leisure to take full advantage of it. A window looked out onto the gantry and nearby workshops. At one end stood a dirty looking radiator, which was always blistering hot. Jim Laws liked to stretch out in the corner by the radiator, which, by common consent, was regarded as his space. Jim was older and bigger than everyone else, and although he never laid claim to any

Murton Colliery in its final days in the early 1990s.

special status, he was looked upon as the senior figure amongst us.

Every so often, Jim, or some other person in that corner of the cabin, would direct a stream of spit on to the radiator, to produce a sizzling sound and cause little bubbles to dance on the surface. The radiator had at one time been painted white, but the grimy atmosphere had turned it an off white, beige colour; on top of which copious amounts of spittle resulted in its being covered in brown stains. All too soon, our brief interlude of leisure would be interrupted by the spasmodic chug of the jigger sending coals down to the belt, and everyone would charge to the door. Your heart sank at the sound.

"Coals commin'!" Kiddo would pipe up, in an irritatingly chirpy voice, as though anyone needed to be apprised of the fact. The next moment, we would be at our places at the belt hurriedly picking stones.

My first pay day came around, and I knew a faint sense of satisfaction at the knowledge that I was earning my own living. My pay for the week was two pounds and ten shillings. My mother let me keep the ten shillings, which I thought was generous as it was double the pocket money I had been receiving in my last year at school.

It was about this time that many people of my age group took up cycling. Not the sporty, competitive type of cycling, or the serious cycling to keep fit kind, but a lazy way of cycling for cycling's sake. Many hours were spent coasting aimlessly around the streets in the evening. At weekends, young people often of only casual acquaintance previously were drawn together in loose bonds of comradeship by the popular pastime, which took them on long jaunts into the great outdoors.

Shiney new bikes in dazzling reds, blues and greens were a familiar sight on the streets. One gold and white machine I thought the most beautiful thing I had ever seen; and, from that time, gold and white became my favourite colour combination. The new bikes were racers, with handle bars that curved under, the sit-up-and-beg type having gone out of fashion by this time. I rode a second-hand bike that Dad had bought for two pounds from someone who lived near the station crossing. It was bigger than all the other bikes, completely black, with motor bike handle bars and corrugated rubber sleeves. The bike had a back peddle brake, which could be daunting until you got used to it. It was a common practice when free wheeling to idly rotate the pedals backwards. If you did that on my bike, the bike would come to an abrupt halt and you would be thrown against the handle bars.

I had mixed feelings about the bike. I envied those of my friends who were mounted upon sparkling new bikes; yet I knew they envied me for the distinctiveness of my machine. The big, black frame and, especially, the motor bike handle bars gave bike and rider an individuality lacking in the others, which, despite the newness of the machines, and the variety of colours, were of a sameness, and I received several requests from those eager to try it out.

A group of Murton cyclists – a little bit before my time.

On Saturdays and Sundays, we ventured into the countryside, cycling sometimes in single file, sometimes two or three abreast, to places like Finchale Abbey, not far out of Durham, which was a favourite destination. The roads then could be free of traffic for miles. It was only the odd motorist that we had to allow for, and which caused us to swerve over to the inside of the road to let him pass. On weekdays, late in the evening, I would cycle up to Calvert Terrace at the top of the Cornfield to drop in on Eddy Ganning. Eddy had been in my class at school, and we had remained friends. But Eddy wasn't the main reason for my excursions into his neighbourhood. Jean Ambler was. Jean lived in the same street as Eddy, and she was the current object of my affections. It was one of those adolescent attractions, bitter-sweet and generally short-lived, begun at school in this case. For a few weeks in the summer, I haunted the place; and I don't think Eddy was fooled into thinking that it was solely our friendship that drew me there.

I had been at my station on the belts for several weeks, toiling hard, when, one day, I was called away and sent to work elsewhere. Why I was chosen, I don't know; perhaps it was because my place at the belt was nearest the foot of the stairs. My new workplace was up the stairs and around the corner from the old, in a great, roofed area where most activity at bank took place. I was assigned to a place at the top of a narrow incline where a wagon way ran between two brick walls. After the tubs had been emptied of their contents, it became my job to couple them together before lowering them down the incline. This was accomplished by dregging them to control their momentum. A dreg was a wooden stake about fifteen inches in length, which, when it was thrust between the spokes of the wheels, acted as a brake, slowing down the motion of the tubs, eventually halting their progress altogether. It was essential to be alert at all times as there was only about a yard between the wagon way and the wall on my side. Sometimes a tub came off the way and had to be lifted back on, a task which ordinarily was not difficult but which was made so by the cramped conditions. Once I had connected about thirty-five to forty chummins, at a given signal I would remove the dregs. The set would then rumble off down the incline and around a bend in the track, where, eventually, they would be shunted into the cage, bound for the shaft bottom and inbye.

I very soon got the hang of my new appointment, which, if it didn't stretch the ability unduly, was nevertheless a lot less boring than labouring all day long at the belt. In the ordinary sense, the Pit Head was a noisy place; compared to the belts, it was a haven of tranquillity. My present duties involved some degree of mobility, and were performed less mechanically and with an added amount of responsibility. I was privileged in a way, and am ashamed to say that I gave no further thought to my erstwhile companions, who were still slaving away on the belts.

Murton Colliery apprentices at Houghton Training Centre. Left to right: Ken Rowe, Jack Chapman, Clive Rodgers, Mr Chicken (supervisor), Ken Sinclair and Jack Lashley.

The foreman in charge of work at bank was Ralph Ridley, who was of my parents' generation, and whom I knew by reputation as a leading light in the Amateur Operatic Society. Ralph was an amiable type of man, rather handsome, of average height, with a broad, powerful physique. He wore a battered old trilby at work, which set him apart from the other surface workers, including myself, whose headgear hardly varied from the soft, peaked cap or "cheesecutter".

Ralph was one of the most active men I knew. He was always on the move, for his responsibility for the smooth running of operations took him to all parts of the workplace, which he covered in quick, deliberate strides. Very infrequently, I enjoyed a short break while awaiting the arrival of chummins at the incline. During one of these quiet spells, I was sitting reading a book when Ralph appeared. He gently reminded me that the Pit Head was no place to be reading books, and that I must be always alert. I felt ashamed at being caught out in that way. He was the boss and I knew that he was right. But I have never been more kindly reprimanded.

After putting in as much time handling tubs as I devoted to the task of culling stones, the day arrived for my transference, together with most of my former workmates, to the Mining Training Centre at Houghton, where all pit boys were sent to prepare them for work underground.

Chapter Three
A Reluctant Thespian

The fact that people today go attired in the ugliest clothes since our ancestors dwelt in caves can be traced to the year, 1952, when jeans first appeared in this country. I am being opinionated, I know. But as this is a testament of my youth, I think I might be allowed to indulge a prejudice or two.

I wasn't always of this opinion; quite the contrary. At the time, I was attending the Miners' Training Centre at Houghton. All my peers were wearing the new jeans, and I pestered my mother daily until she bought me a pair. Every morning, I could hardly wait to put them on. It must have been the only time in my working life when I did not wake up hating the sound of the alarm clock, but instead, rose from my bed with a glad heart in anticipation of the day ahead. Because it meant I would be wearing my new jeans. Jeans came in different shades of blue. Some were of a very light shade; but mine were of the darkest blue, which I liked best, even though my mother had chosen them and not me. Like the trousers that were worn then, jeans had turn ups; so they looked all the more like what essentially they are, work clothes.

I journeyed to the training centre at Houghton by the regular bus service, as did the pit lads from the villages around, except, of course, those who lived in Houghton.

Houghton Colliery, across the road from the Training Centre.

For them, it was but a short walk to work. Eventually, a miners' training centre was opened at Seaham; but it didn't exist then. The Houghton centre was located on the road to Newbottle, in the shadow of a promontory of naked rock, which, from certain vantage points, was visible for many miles distant. The building could easily have been mistaken for a primary school, and, for all I know, it might once have served some such purpose. It was a rather featureless structure, with a couple of classrooms looking out onto a walled yard; a playground, you would have called it, if it had been a conventional school. At the morning and afternoon break, the trainees would be let out into the yard to stretch their legs, and, in the case of not a few, to enjoy a cigarette. It is many years since the building stood by the side of the road. A car sales business stands there now. The Pit Head straggled the margin of the road on the opposite side. Houghton was one of the oldest pits in the county. Like the training centre above ground, it served as a place

Where Houghton Miners Training Centre once stood.

of instruction for trainees, giving practical experience to complement the theory absorbed in the classroom. And, like the training centre, it has long passed out of existence.

The training programme required that three days in the week be spent in the classroom and two days down the pit. The following week, the allocation of days to classroom and pit would be reversed. In class, lectures were given on basic mining practise. We weren't given much to write, and I don't recall being given any reading matter. The instructors were experienced miners, who treated us like adults and not like schoolboys, which I think was greatly appreciated. Still, there were those who grumbled about being back at school and having to sit at desks and have questions put to them. I was bored a lot of the time. Even so, I think I was in a small minority, if not alone, amongst those of my intake, in preferring the classroom to the pit. Some seemed to anticipate their introduction to work underground in a spirit of adventure. At midday, dinner was served in the Newbottle pit canteen, a few yards up the road. The food was poor, certainly when compared to home cooking, but also to the standard of food dished up in the Murton pit canteen. Afterwards, a stroll down the road to an ice cream shop on the main street was usually on the cards. The shop was popular for selling hot fruit drinks.

Of the events of my first day underground I have no clear recollection, beyond one or two stand out impressions. I recall clambering into the pit cage for the first time and seeing the daylight suddenly extinguished and the scene at bank disappear from view in that downward rush into the void. I am not quite sure what I expected to find when I stepped out into the light at the shaft bottom. Not coal that had yet to be mined, for I knew that the coal face was far inbye. But I was not prepared for the sense of height and space, or for such an intense scene of industry. And utterly unexpected and seeming strange, were such things as electric lighting, telephones, and whitewashed brick walls.

My time at Houghton Training Centre lasted from the autumn of 1952 until the January of the following year. At the end of the course, I was awarded an NCB certificate, which for some obscure reason I have ever since kept, attesting to my eligibility to be employed underground in a coal mine.

A National Coal Board Certificate of Training from 1953.

Jeans were not the only American import of 1952. That was also the year of the square dance. It would be stretching it a bit to say that there was a square dancing craze, but it enjoyed a modest, if short-lived, fashion. Classes were started up in many parts, and for a while, people in England were do-se-do-ing and swingin' their pardners to whoops of glee in bizarre parody of American country bumpkins. By the end of the year, square dancing was a spent force, and it remains a forgotten episode in fifties cultural history. Sixty years down the line, and the ubiquitous denim shows no sign of going out of fashion.

My participation in the American-inspired pastime was as brief as it was surprising; but it led on to something that proved to be of more lasting interest. At the time, I was associating with Noreen Debbage, a girl I had known from schooldays, who had been in my class, in fact, although she was about twenty months younger than me. Noreen was the successor to Jean. It was another of those adolescent courtships (moderns might still find that word in the dictionary), in this case carried over from school, and enduring for about ten weeks, which, in terms of adolescent courtships, should count as a diamond jubilee.

Before me, Noreen had been seeing John Booth, a boy of my own age whom I came to know and like. The two of them grew up together in the same street in Cornwall. Unfortunately, Noreen could never make up her mind which of us she would rather be with, John or me. But for a long while, relatively long, that is, it was me; and it was during this time that Noreen got me into square dancing.

A class was being taught in the Council Schools by Sheila Kirby, a local woman. Sheila was a voice and drama coach, who would be in her late twenties when I became associated with her. She was attractive, with a good singing voice and more than passable acting ability; all of which made her a natural for the lead roles in the Amateur Operatic Society productions. When she was not so engaged, Sheila ran

Sheila Kirby in a performance of Murton Amateur Operatic Society.

the Murton Youth Choral and Drama Club, which was her own creation. The square dancing was a side interest, enthusiasm for which Sheila had succeeded in passing on to the young people in her society. Noreen heard about it and was keen, so I was coaxed into joining as her dance partner, and became only the second male member of the square dancing troupe.

Sheila's portable gramophone supplied the music, and, having previously demonstrated and rehearsed the sequences, Sheila called them out in her dulcet tones, declining to attempt the hillbilly twang affected by other aficionados. People threw themselves into the new recreation with gusto. The steps were surprisingly easy to master. In no time at all, I was rollicking with the best of them, to the point where I was able to

Sheila commands her Drama Club troops.

overcome my natural reserve and let out a few whoops myself.

Enthusiasm for the trans-Atlantic fad faded about the time that the romance faded. I think Noreen went back to John. Or perhaps she took a breather from the both of us. Or perhaps John, like me, was happy to take a breather from someone who displayed a near pathological inability to make up her mind as to whom she would rather be with. As for Sheila, she now concentrated her energies on the Choral and Drama Club, which, by a chance combination of circumstances, claimed my interest also.

When on that first evening I joined the square dancing class, I thought Sheila regarded me as nothing more than someone making up the numbers. I could not have guessed that she saw me as the answer to a prayer. The show currently in production was a revue, incorporating choral and dance routines and a one act play, There's No Problem, which, among the mainly female cast, included two male characters. One of these roles was being played by Jack Pringle, the only male member of the company; and although the other role was miniscule, it wasn't really feasible to have a girl play it. The Murton Youth Choral and Drama Club was beset by a problem familiar to many amateur companies at that time, a shortage of male members.

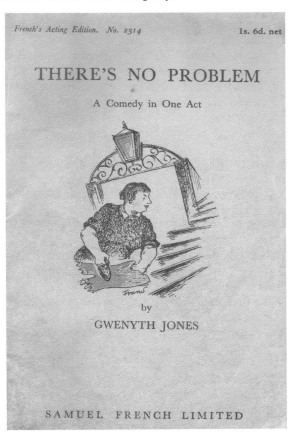

The cover of the one act play There's No Problem.

Sheila used all her considerable powers of persuasion to get me to take on the role. Rather unfairly, she gave to believe that the success of the entire production depended upon my cooperation in the matter. How she would have resolved her difficulty if I had not happened along I can only guess. She would probably have had to use a girl in the part. Finally, I capitulated, and, not without some misgiving, agreed to do it. The play was a North Country domestic comedy, typical of its kind, low brow and cliché-ridden.

I was entrusted with the part of the boyfriend of the teenage daughter, who was played in vivacious style by Brenda Johnson. All one act comedies seemed to feature a teenage daughter; and there was usually a boyfriend. My role required little acting skill, and not much in the way of a rehearsal. I had two lines: "Evenin'!" As I was dragged on stage by Brenda to meet the family; and "Evenin'!" as I was dragged off stage thirty seconds later. I practiced saying the word, endeavouring to give a different intonation each time. But there are only so many ways you can say "Evenin'!" The show was performed in the Miners' Hall on three consecutive nights, and was well attended every night. It was deemed an unqualified success, not unexpectedly, for Sheila enjoyed a high reputation as a producer, and she had assembled a talented troupe of young performers.

Having done my bit to ensure the success of the show, I prepared to depart. But Sheila had other ideas. She was now confidant that she had got hold of her second male member of the company. An ambitious dramatic production was projected for the coming season, the three act play, Bonaventure, in which Sheila herself was to play a leading role. There were two male parts, both sizeable. Jack was given the crucial role of a homicidal doctor, which took him on and off stage for the duration of the play, and placed him at centre stage for the denouement in the final scene. Sheila was again at her persuasive best, all sweetness and charm, in order to recruit me to the cause. Without me for the other male role the play couldn't be put on, as she was at pains to point out. I was putty in her hands. So began my apprenticeship to Thespis.

Sheila was adept at instilling confidence. She assured me I hadn't a thing to worry about; that I was perfect for the part. The part was that of slack-jawed, slow speaking

Willy Pentridge, a simpleton. I think the audience twigged this the moment I uttered my first line: "Ah, floods be out. 'Tis always cold when floods be out." I entered stage right and shuffled across to the fireplace stage left, bearing an armful of logs for the fire. I dropped one on Moira Denning's foot and she hopped about on the other foot and yelped "You clumsy oaf!" The audience thought it was in the script.

The plot revolved around a woman falsely accused of murder who is detained in a convent near Norwich, where the real murderer also resides. As the story unfolds, a strong relationship develops between the accused woman, Sarat Carne, played with great feeling by Sheila, and the saintly Sister Mary Bonaventure, played with equal competence by Maureen Stokoe. The daughter of the manager of Thompson's Red Stamp Stores on the Terrace, Maureen was a prominent actress in the troupe. To heighten the pathos of the drama, Sheila added offstage background music, the moving Intermezzo from Cavaleria Rusticana, to which someone at some time had added words.

Sheila's production of Bonaventure came in for a lot of praise, some of it aimed in my direction. I learned then what I have at other times observed, that feigned idiocy will win plaudits when often more subtle portrayals go unappreciated. I believe John Mills once won an Academy Award for playing a village idiot. Many of his, always accomplished, roles were deserving of as much. Jack Pringle gave an exceptional, nuanced interpretation as the plausible but sinister doctor, and I never thought he was given the credit he deserved. It was generally assumed that he would always contribute a faultless performance, and that was the measure of his ability as an actor. I think Jack hailed from South Hetton. He was a trained tenor, and, like Sheila, active in the Operatic Society, taking on featured roles in operettas. After the Bonaventure production, Jack, together with a number of older girls, left the company. His defection left me as the only male performer for Sheila to call upon, and a largely inexperienced one at that.

With my friend Albert Swan (left) over the park.

Sheila's next production was another revue. The one act play selected for our performance was a complete contrast to the usual working class melodramas. Instead, the action centred upon the problems of an aristocratic family living in a country manor. The role of the family lawyer was assigned to me. It was a million miles from reality. Picture John Geilgud as an Australian sheep shearer. It was about that far. In an effort to appear convincing, I affected a high pitched, nasal delivery and a pompous manner. I thought it effective, and Sheila had no complaints about my interpretation of the part. I can still recall my first line, uttered when declining a glass of sherry. "Many thanks but no. On the subject of sherry, my doctor and I do not, alas, see eye to eye." I must emphasize that I merely spoke the words; I didn't write them. Dad was in the audience for the first night. He said I was good. But he would.

Cliffy Nichols – another good friend.

Now that I had become a fixture in the society, I was keen to interest others who might take some of the burden off my shoulders. So I managed to persuade two of my closest friends, Albert Swan and Cliffy Nichols, to join the troupe, for which service Sheila was profoundly grateful. She now enjoyed what was something of a luxury in having three male performers to call upon; and it made the company more rounded. There were not many regional one act plays of the type we put on that had more than three male parts. About the same time, a number of new, young faces were to be seen among the girls in the company. Being a relatively seasoned performer by this time, I got to play the browbeaten husbands and stressed fathers which were a staple of one act comedies. Joan Cowley, who

22

lived in the same street as me, was usually cast as my opposite number and nemesis. The boyfriend parts now went to either Cliffy or Albert. I think Albert took to the life of the Choral and Drama Club more earnestly than Cliffy. He became serious about singing and went privately to Sheila for voice lessons.

One of the plays with which we scored a notable triumph was When the Old Cock Crows. An incorrigible ne'er-do-well comes under the lash of a shrew's tongue for leading astray an impressionable young man and his nice girlfriend. Joan and I were the feuding couple, Albert played the part of the impressionable young man, and Margaret Doust was the girlfriend. The show ran for three successive nights in the Miners' Hall, after which we thought we had done with it. Then Sheila revealed that she had entered our little comedy in a forthcoming festival of one act plays, which was to take place in the Rock House community theatre in Seaham, three miles away. It was actually a competition. At the end of the night, one of the plays would be judged to have won, and the cast of players would be required to reprise their performances in a theatre in Durham at a later date.

When we were not on stage ourselves, we were able to run an eye over the opposition. It appeared to me that we had as good a chance as any of the other drama societies of emerging on top. In the event, to our huge delight, When the Old Cock Crows was judged to be the winning entrant. Of course, it was a feather in the cap of the successful producer, and Sheila could hardly conceal her pleasure at the outcome. We took the play to Durham, Sheila and the whole cast travelling there and back by service bus, and performed it before an audience of theatre people, who seemed most appreciative.

My farewell performance was as a beleaguered father in the comedy, Haste to the Wedding. Described on the front cover of the book as "a rural scurry", the play focuses upon

The Sixth Production of

Murton Youth Choral and Drama Club

in The Miners' Hall, Murton

TUESDAY FEBRUARY 28th

at 7-15 p.m. prompt

Produced and Musically Directed by
SHEILA A. KIRBY, L.R.A.M. (Mus.) A.T.C.L. (Eloc.)

Pianist	Ethel Moor, A.L.C.M.
Secretary and Treasurer	Maisie L. Richardson
Stage Managers	Jack Richardson and James Toft

Admission by Programme 2/-

Children Half Price

R. Hindhaugh, Printer, Murton

A programme for the Drama Club's sixth production.

an ordinary working class family thrown into turmoil by the impending marriage of the elder daughter. I was handed the part of the hapless head of the household, Sam Barcham. Joan Cowley essayed the role of the long-suffering wife, and Albert appeared as the implausibly named Jonathon Tuttle, father of the groom-to-be and my drinking mate. There was no boyfriend role, and, oddly, the bride-to-be, Gwendoline, was never seen, being occupied upstairs all the time, trying on her wedding dress or otherwise engaged in pre-nuptial matters. There was a lively, younger daughter, played by Margaret White, and a complaining, misery guts of a grandmother, played by Maureen Kirby. Pat Finan and Maureen Hewitson, playing the parts of two busybody neighbours, made up the cast. An audience of about a hundred and fifty turned up nightly to see the performance.

Haste to the Wedding formed part of the sixth production of the Murton Youth Choral and Drama Club. The production marked the end of my association with the society. There may have been another show, but it was not long after I had tendered my farewells that Sheila met her future husband, and, following her marriage, went to live in Switzerland.

3. "Haste to the Wedding"

A Comedy In One Act

Samuel Barcham	Peter Bartley
Mrs. Barcham	Joan Cowley
Florrie	Margaret White
Grandma Barcham	Maureen Kirby
Mrs. Pilbeam	Pat Finan
Mrs. Blick	Maureen Hewitson
Jonathan Tuttle	Albert Swan

(Scene : The kitchen of the Barcham's Cottage, on the morning of their eldest daughter's wedding)

Short Interval

The cast of a typical one act rural comedy.

Chapter Four
Hooray for Hollywood

Every person is conscious, to a greater or lesser extent, of the influences shaping his life – family, profession, place of origin, are three rather obvious examples. In my own case, and I've no doubt it applies to others, there is something which has influenced my life in subtler ways, and which has continued to give me great pleasure while making no particular demands on my loyalty, unlike the aforementioned, and being somewhat frivolous in comparison. Am I being too mysterious? I will come to the point, since it forms the subject matter of the present chapter.

The Hollywood film industry, although extending over many decades, was really a phenomenon of my generation and my parents' generation. There was, of course, a British film industry; almost every country has had a film industry. But for half a century, Hollywood was the undisputed capital, the dream factory for millions, whose stars were idolized like no public figures before or since. The heyday of Hollywood spanned barely twenty-five years, roughly from the early thirties to the mid fifties. The advent of television and the end of the studio system might have killed off the industry; but it revived to some extent, even if its greatest achievements were all in the past.

The Empire when it was a bingo hall.

The attraction of the pictures isn't difficult to understand. People everywhere and at all times love a story. And the cinema must be the best means ever devised for telling a story. You can visualize a story in your imagination with the aid of a book, or see a story represented in a highly stylized manner on stage; but in the cinema the story unfolds before your eyes in a uniquely realistic way. Then, the allure surrounding the performers who acted out the stories was very powerful. A mediocre film might get by depending on the popularity of its stars. Sometimes I thought I would like to be a great character actor like Charles Laughton. At other times, I wanted to be a two-fisted hero like John Wayne. I wanted to be able to put over a song like Bing Crosby and dance like Donald O'Connor, be as debonair as William Powell or as self-possessed as James Cagney, a performer who acted with his whole body.

Although the glamour and sophistication of the film capital was very far removed from my experience, and that of everyone I knew, nonetheless, Hollywood cast its influence over our lives in diverse ways. Clothes, hair styles, make-up, courting techniques, the language in which some people expressed themselves, even the way they smoked a cigarette, all owed something to Hollywood. In the film, It Happened One Night, Clark Gable removed his shirt to reveal that he wore nothing underneath. Almost overnight, sales of men's undershirts in America plummeted. During the war, many women worked in factories operating machines. To avoid their hair getting caught in the machinery, they wore turbans, a precaution necessitated by the peek-a-boo hairstyle favoured by Hollywood actress, Veronica Lake, and copied by women the world over. We knew every star and supporting actor by name and spoke of them almost as though they were personal acquaintances. In some strange way they became our property.

It was indicative of the phenomenal popularity of Hollywood films that a pit village like Murton could have three cinemas. The programmes were changed in mid week, and on Saturday night all three cinemas had two houses, that is, consecutive performances. You could expect a near full house everywhere on Saturday night. Business was slow if, at other times, the house was anything less than half full. A much-heralded epic entertainment like Gone with the Wind would be booked for the whole week, and every night would be a sell out. At such times, it was common to see people turned away and the full sign put up, Sunday night was the occasion for showing old films, which afforded an opportunity for a second viewing of particular favourites that had been enjoyed the first time around.

Tucked away in the hollow between the High House and the Northern bus depot, was Murton's oldest picture house, the Olympia. In addition to screening films, the Olympia was at one time the venue for variety shows. My mother, together with her sister and brother appeared on stage in the Olympia in a 1920s school production. According to Dad, the famous strongman and world champion heavyweight wrestler, Georg Hackenschmidt once performed there.

It is probably true to say that the Olympia was the most downmarket of Murton's three cinemas. Fate had decreed, not inappropriately, it seemed, that it should be located at the lowest point in Murton. Some called it a flea pit, though it was far from being that. It was of a reasonable size, though not as big as the other two, and had an upstairs circle. Where it lagged behind the Empire and the Rex was in a certain

Children taking part in a production at the Olympia in the 1920s.

disregard for the comfort of its patrons. Although they were keen picture goers, I don't ever recall my parents frequenting the Olympia. Only rarely were the top films of the day screened there. The featured pictures were generally the products of the minor Hollywood studios. The floor of the auditorium was level, making it difficult to see the screen if you were unfortunate enough to have someone tall sitting in front of you. Sometime in the fifties, a new floor with a gradient was put in, which improved the Olympia's image, if only slightly.

Were it not for children, who always figured large among the downstairs clientele, the Olympia might well have gone out of business. Consequently, there was always a restless atmosphere. The diminutive, nimble-footed usher, Mr Knox, Jonty to everyone, was kept busy patrolling the centre aisle keeping order. He could be as loud as the individuals he endeavoured to control, which rather defeated the purpose. "Hey, you, sit down!" from time to time his voice would crackle above the soundtrack of the picture, while he flashed his torch at the offending party. Then he would turn on his heel to admonish a

Georg Hackenschmidt.

group of miscreants on the other side. "Be quiet, you lot! Turn around! Watch the picture." It was bad enough that the paying customers had to put up with a fidgety audience comprised mostly of juveniles, they had also to put up with Jonty periodically barking reproofs across the auditorium, which, you half imagined, made the figures on the screen start. But in all fairness, no one would have envied Jonty his job.

Visually more pleasing than its rivals, the Rex was the newest of the three cinemas, dating from 1939, the year war broke out. Hollywood was at its zenith; many considered it the most productive year in the history of film making. Pictures released in 1939 included Gone With the Wind, The Wizard of Oz, Goodbye Mr Chips, The Roaring Twenties, Gunga Din and Mr Smith goes to Washington, all top draw attractions.

The Rex was a massive, brick edifice, which, as has already been said, occupied a dominant position on the crest of a hill. It was approached from the main road by multiple flights of steps, which had the appearance of terracing seen at Football League grounds. Children would sit balancing on the rails and slide all the way to the bottom. If the featured picture was a big draw, people would queue on the steps while waiting to be admitted.

The Rex had by far the most impressive foyer, high and wide, with the ticket office commanding the centre. From the foyer, two flights of stairs, one on either side, with a right angle turn half way up ascended to a broad verandah, which gave admittance to the upstairs seating. The stalls were accessed at the rear of the foyer by a door three steps down, in each corner. Oddly situated at the front of the stalls where the normal seating ended, were a half dozen or so wooden benches, that looked like, and might once have been, church pews. Children who had been admitted for half price were shown to these seats when the house was full.

A poster for Gone With the Wind.

If you were one of the last to gain admittance and were obliged to sit in the front pew, you could stretch out a leg and touch the panel of the orchestra pit with your foot. To view the screen, it was necessary to tilt your head back at an acute angle, which put a strain both on the neck and on the eyes. From such close proximity, the figures on the screen appeared giant sized. The regular cinema usher, Mr Lambton, lived only yards from the building. He was mostly kept occupied in showing patrons to the available seating, perhaps occasionally casting a reproving glance at someone about to step out of line. But downstairs in the Rex, unlike in the Olympia, wasn't much troubled by rowdies.

The Rex displayed the films of Universal Studios, later Universal International, Republic Pictures, and the J Arthur Rank organization. Many of John Wayne's pictures were screened at the Rex, as were the comedies of the top box office draw, Abbott and Costello. While it existed, the Rex was the regular home of the Amateur Operatic Society. It had all the advantages of a good theatre – a large seating capacity with

John Wayne and the poster for one of his most popular films – The Searchers.

unimpeded viewing, a deep stage and spacious wings, an orchestra pit, and dressing rooms to the rear of the stage. The relatively short life span of the building is much to be regretted.

If you were to pass Stobie's shop at the bottom of the Terrace and turn right by the corner of the Colliery Inn, you would be facing the front of the Empire. First impressions can be indelible, so I must emphasize that the interior of the Empire left nothing to be desired, and gave the lie to the impression engendered by the exterior, which, in situation and appearance was unprepossessing, if not drab. Stills of the main picture currently being shown, and of coming attractions, could be viewed in the window of the adjoining box office. There were two or three steps to negotiate at the entrance, and, once inside the swing doors, several more steps before facing the ticket office. The ticket office was central to the small foyer, small, that is, when compared to the foyer of the Rex. Framed photographs of Hollywood stars looked down from the walls.

The Empire had the edge on the other two cinemas in terms of comfort and the quality of films it offered. The circle seats were more luxurious than in any of the picture palaces of Sunderland, or in any others of my experience. Pictures screened at the Empire were the output of major studios such as Warner Brothers, Twentieth Century Fox and, biggest of all, MGM, generally acknowledged to be the pre-eminent Hollywood studio. The Empire, like the Rex, was a place where a man might take his wife, certainly in preference to the Olympia. It is many years since pictures were screened at the Empire. Like many of the luxury picture palaces of the era, it was fated to become a bingo hall. Closed for a time, it has recently been demolished.

RITZ : SUNDERLAND

Monday, May 3rd ———————— for six days
PLEASE WATCH SCREEN AND PRESS FOR THIS WEEK'S ATTRACTION

Monday, May 10th ———————— for six days
CINEMASCOPE
Guy Madison, Joan Weldon and James Whitmore in
THE COMMAND ⓤ
(WarnerColor)
also full supporting programme

Monday, May 17th ———————— for six days
PLEASE WATCH SCREEN AND PRESS FOR THIS WEEK'S ATTRACTION

Monday, May 24th ———————— for six days
Dirk Bogarde, Denholm Elliott and Akim Tamiroff in
THEY WHO DARE ⓤ
(Technicolor)
Also WELCOME THE QUEEN (in Color) ⓤ

Monday, May 31st ———————— for six days
Marlon Brando, James Mason, Deborah Kerr,
Greer Garson, John Gielgud and Louis Calhern in
JULIUS CAESAR ⓤ
Also : Foxhunter—Champion Jumper ⓤ

SUNDAYS AT THE RITZ

———————— Sunday, May 9th ————————
Robert Cummings, Joan Caulfield Girl Of The Year (Tech.) Ⓐ
John Ireland .... The Rebel Ⓐ
———————— Sunday, May 16th ————————
John Wayne, Patricia Neal .... Operation Pacific ⓤ
Robert Alda .... Hollywood Varieties ⓤ
———————— Sunday, May 23rd ————————
Red Skelton, Brian Donlevy, Arlene Dahl .... My Hero ⓤ
Richard Denning, Audrey Long ... Insurance Investigator Ⓐ
———————— Sunday, May 30th ————————
Preston Foster, Lynn Bari .... Secret Agent Of Japan Ⓐ
Albert Modley, Mai Bacon .... Up For The Cup ⓤ

Programmes are liable to alteration

The Perfect Gift — AN ABC CINEMA SEAT TOKEN

A programme for the ABC Cinema, Sunderland in 1953.

The cinema programme at the time adhered to a format which hardly varied from one place to the next. In the 1940s, the double bill, featuring an 'A' picture and a 'B' picture, was a fairly universal arrangement. The supporting picture would very often be one of a series, such as the Sherlock Holmes or Charlie Chan mysteries. In the 1950s, inane comedies like Ma and Pa Kettle and Francis the talking Mule achieved favour with 'B' picture audiences. The double feature format was beginning to disappear by then, possibly because many new feature films were of an inordinate length. If there was no 'B' picture, and sometimes even if there was one, the agenda would typically be comprised of a cartoon, which at the Empire was usually Donald Duck, a news bulletin such as Pathe or Movietone News, and the trailer for the forthcoming week.

Sometimes the cartoon would be replaced by what most people called a traveltalk, but what in film books are referred to as travelogues. The traveltalk was a two reel entertainment in documentary style. It could be purely escapist, but could sometimes be serious, as in the case of The March of Time. The Rex got the British black and white traveltalks of Jean and Ronald Haines, which portrayed the everyday working life of the people of some European country, and were distinguished by their quaint, rural settings. Cottage industries featured a lot. A typical scene depicted a peasant weaving outside the open door of his cottage. The films were insightful in an unglamorous way, for this was before the invasion of Europe by British holidaymakers, when there still existed a mystique about foreign countries. Each film was narrated in the mellifluous tones of BBC newsreader, Frank Phillips.

The Fitzpatrick traveltalks screened at the Empire were glossy American offerings, noted for their brilliant colours, exotic locations and abundance of tropical flowers. They were hated by film critics, who thought them banal. A typical Fitzpatrick traveltalk would end with twilight descending on some tropical paradise and the voice on the soundtrack wistfully intoning the words, "And as the sun slowly sets over the horizon, so we bid farewell to this land of sun, sea and flowers." Fitzpatrick, who had other directorial credits in Hollywood, was recalled with affection and faint amusement by his colleagues in the industry as James, And so we say Farewell, Fitzpatrick. I loved the Fitzpatrick traveltalks, and I didn't care what film critics thought of them.

Before I turned fifteen, there was one day every week when I stopped off at Jimmy Anderson's paper shop on my way home from school to pick up my Boys' Adventure weeklies, the Wizard and the Hotspur. The shop was half a mile straight down the road from school, next to St Paul's church. The shop would be full of boys at the time, for although the magazines went on the paper bill and could have been delivered to the house, we couldn't wait to snap them up immediately they were conveyed to the shop.

A year or two later, I was still a regular caller at the paper shop; only this time it was film magazines that claimed my interest. I had a regular order for Picturegoer and Picture Show, both of which I read from cover to cover. In addition to articles of general interest to film buffs, both publications furnished a weekly review of pictures currently on release. The Picture Show tended to concentrate on British films, and was invaluable in that it supplied the cast list and other credits of every film it reviewed. The Picturegoer focussed very much on Hollywood and its latest output.

Most Saturdays about midday, I walked to the Police Station or the Store Clock and boarded the number twenty one bus to Sunderland. With stops, the journey took about twenty-five minutes, twenty if not many people got on or off. The Northern bus en route from Murton to Sunderland left sometimes from Easington Lane, sometimes from as far afield as Thornley, picking up passengers along the way. It pulled up at Park Lane near the short cut entrance to Holmside, which today passes a mini market. A pie stall stood to the side and the Economic bus usually

An advert for Anderson's shop and one of the comics they sold – The Hotspur.

SIX STORIES AND A PICTURE-STORY—THIS WEEK AND EVERY WEEK!

THE HOTSPUR
EVERY THURSDAY   PRICE 3d

READ ABOUT THIS
BATTLING REDSKIN
IN THE TERRIFIC BOXING YARN
THE SECRET SIX

parked in front of that. As Sunderland had no bus station then, passengers queued out in the open, in the broad expanse of Park Lane. There were no platforms and no destination signs. Everyone knew where to queue for the bus.

I was bound for the Ritz or the Regal, though sometimes I would head for one of the town's lesser picture houses if it was showing a picture I particularly wanted to see. Kiddo was a film fan like me, and sometimes we met up by prior arrangement; but often I went alone, stocking up on sweets, usually Payne's Poppets or sugared almonds. Near the Palatine, there was a little, family-run grocer's shop that sold salted nuts, weighed and bagged in the shop. This was long before salted nuts caught on.

The Ritz and the Regal, subsequently the ABC and the Odeon, generally got the best pictures; although I once saw a reissue of Pride and Prejudice somewhere else, and the Picture House in High Street somehow managed to land the hit Ethel Merman musical, There's No Business like Show Business. Considering that the Picture House was widely known as The Ranch on account of the number of westerns shown there, this must have been something of a coup. I once paid the top price of four shillings to sit in the circle of the Ritz, where a Donald O'Connor picture was the main feature. Donald O'Connor was a special favourite of mine. He was an all-round entertainer, who later composed music for symphony orchestras; but mostly I admired him for his dancing ability. James Cagney, who was an accomplished dancer himself, rated Donald O'Connor the best dancer in the business after Fred Astaire and Gene Kelly.

The Ritz or the ABC Cinema, Sunderland.

On Saturday night in Murton, the first house at all three cinemas began at six o' clock, an hour earlier than the beginning of the mid week programme. On returning from Sunderland, I would have my tea, then it was not unusual for me to catch the first house at, say, the Olympia, before dashing across to the Empire for the second house. On a Saturday night, many among my age group, male and female, were drawn to the second house at the Empire. After the programme had ended and the Empire had closed its doors, the young people gathered at the top of the Terrace by the Independent Methodist Church, reluctant to go home. Crowds of perhaps seventy and upwards thronged both sides of the road, spilling over into the middle, talking and laughing, many enjoying a cigarette. The place was wholly ours, as by then the buses had stopped running and there was no other traffic to worry about. There was never a police presence, for a police presence wasn't required, and, in any case, the station was only yards away.

We did nothing much but talk amongst ourselves, and perhaps discuss the film we had just seen. Friends would perhaps arrange to meet the following day, which was Sunday. In my case, friends like Cliffy Nichols, whom I had associated with almost from the time I learnt to walk; and Nicky Jobe, who could produce a witticism at the drop of a hat, and who would confide to us his ideas for short stories that he never got to write.

From time to time, Cliffy, or Nick, or myself would suggest a walk. Then we would amble down the Terrace as far as Stobie's bottom shop, at which point we would turn around and walk slowly back, passing people with the same idea journeying in the opposite direction. This performance would be repeated at least once before the end of the night. In some such observance young people have always kept common company. Chilling out, my grandchildren call it. After a while, when the pleasure dimmed, people would begin to drift away in ones and twos, some directing their steps towards the huddled rows of Cornwall, others to one or other of the streets west of the Terrace. By midnight, everyone would be home and the Terrace deserted.

Chapter Five
The South Drifts

When still only fifteen, I began work in the Five Quarter seam at Murton Colliery, in a place called the South Drifts. To work shifts, you had to be sixteen, so until my sixteenth birthday came along I was restricted to the back shift. In other spheres of industry, and in places like hospitals and fire stations, this would be known as day shift.

The South Drifts was estimated to be 1,200 feet beneath the Easington Greyhound Stadium. Three miles inbye from the pit shaft, the whole distance had to be covered on foot. From the moment of stepping out of the pit cage at the shaft bottom to when work actually began at the workplace, roughly an hour had gone by. I travelled with the power loaders and datal workers who were employed in the same district as me, marras, as I

Easington Greyhound Stadium.

thought of them. We departed at different times from the shaft bottom, depending on whether you caught the first cage or the second. We filled both decks of the cage, squatting shoulder to shoulder in the cramped space. It was an uncomfortable, if mercifully short, descent; for we were obliged to sit on the iron rails on the floor of the cage, which, at other times, supported tubs. When the onsetter opened the gate at the bottom, we were glad to scramble out into the light and stretch our legs. It would be some time before any of us would again be able to stand fully upright.

From the bright, almost cheery, atmosphere of the shaft bottom, with its whitewashed walls and snug onsetter's cabin, the road plunged into a gloomy interior, twisting and turning between rows of broken, off centre props, through low-roofed galleries that had first been excavated in the 1880s. Eons ago, it seemed, yet the pit then had almost a third of its working life behind it. We walked bent double, in single file, kicking up stone dust as we went; men uniformly kitted out. A bait tin slapped against one thigh; slung over the shoulder, or else affixed to the belt on the other side, was the precious water bottle. Battery lamps, our sole source of light now, were carried in the hand, which was held out in front so as to shed light on the ground ahead. The battery that powered the lamp sat in a pouch, which was attached to the belt at the back. Once inbye, the lamp would slot into the front of the helmet, so leaving both hands free for work. Only the deputy in charge of the flat carried an oil lamp, which he used on occasions to test for the presence of gas.

For the first part of the journey, the road followed an old wagon way that had long since served its purpose. Seemingly, no one had thought it worth the trouble to have it dismantled and removed, and there frequently

Murton pit shaft – from here it was three miles to the South Drifts.

At the coal face – Murton Colliery in 1977.

was heard a muttered curse as someone stumbled over it. The roof was not of a uniform height, something I found particularly troublesome. Only rarely did I cover the distance inbye without at least once banging my head against it. Sometimes I collided with it so violently my pit helmet would become dislodged from my head in the collision. The helmet spared me many injuries; but the sudden jolt to the neck was unpleasant, resulting in a salvo of curses being called down upon the offending segment of roof.

Periodically along the route, a flash of the lamp would reveal the entrance to some long abandoned gallery; an old roadway, perhaps. I could never succeed in suppressing a shiver at the thought of men generations past who had once toiled there. You might almost hear their voices, above the thud of picks and the rasp of the shovel. The beam from the lamp could reach no further than a few yards into the cavernous interior, allowing no more than the briefest of glances before pressing on. After trekking for more than a mile, a ventilation door appeared, and, on passing through it, we left behind this labyrinth of extinct workings with its ghostly echoes of the past.

A long climb to the top of a drift road lay ahead. There was ample headroom on this leg of the journey, so for the first time since leaving the shaft bottom we could walk erect. As we plodded on, the air became fresher and cooler. We emerged at the top of the drift, where we came upon the first signs of industry. Tubs routinely passed this way, towed in both directions. For we were now entered upon the main road that connected the mine workings inbye, with the shaft outbye at the place where coals were drawn. Never once pausing in our stride, we struck out along the narrow verge separating the wall of coal and stone on our left and the wagon way to the right. At more or less regular intervals, we passed the refuge holes that had been hollowed out of the wall, about the height of a man and deep enough to accommodate perhaps two men of average bulk, should any emergency require their use. It was the last leg of our journey inbye; a long one. After a while, lights would be seen flickering in the distance. Some of the first shift lads on their way outbye. In a few minutes, we would be level with them, and some good natured banter would pass between us before they were gone. No one ever stopped. We talked as we walked. They were always in a hurry, impatient to be home. That would be us several hours from now. We pressed on, our objective a pin point of light dead ahead. The road seemed never ending; but every time we looked up, the ray of light had grown bigger, until at last we came upon a busy, well-lit junction.

Pausing for only a moment to exchange a few words of greeting with the two men who were normally stationed here, we made a right turn at the junction and entered a high-ceilinged gallery with a double wagon way. Another two minutes walk brought us to where Mr Coxon, the deputy in charge of the district, had his kist. The word is very old, believed to be Viking in origin, and means chest or box. Here were kept the deputy's report book, first aid equipment, various tools, and whatever else the deputy might require in the performance of his duties. Mr Coxon was the first deputy I worked under. He had identical twin sons, John and George, who were of my own age, and who also worked in the South Drifts. Years ago, when I was no older than eleven, I got into a fight with one of them in the queue for the Saturday afternoon matinee at the Rex. I don't know which one, for until I came to work with them I could never tell them apart. And I have no idea what the fight was about. Now, seeing one another every day, the three of us soon became great friends.

The deputy's kist was the assembly point where all the men reported for instructions prior to the commencement of work, and where the deputy would examine their lamps before they moved on. The brakeman who operated the main and tail system went and sat at his haulage engine. Across the wagon way opposite, empty tubs stood at the loader waiting to be filled. It was well lit here, but the lighting extended no further. The power loaders took a right angled turn at the loader and disappeared into the darkness, which, for a few seconds only, was pierced by the glint of their lamps. They proceeded along a narrow trail for perhaps eighty or a hundred yards, before arriving at the coal face. I went no further than the area of the loader and the main and tail engine, for this was where I functioned as a landing lad.

'Darkie' – The last pony to come up from Murton Pit.

The main and tail was a means of hauling tubs which had been linked together in sets of forty and upwards. The system involved the use of two wire, cable ropes, and was ingeniously simple. The main rope was affixed to the front tub of the set and the tail rope to the last tub. At an appointed signal, the breaker inbye would start up his haulage engine, and, as the rope coiled around the drum on the engine, the set of chummins would be hauled inbye from the shaft bottom. Once the set arrived at the landing, the two ropes would be disconnected. The tail rope would then become the main rope and the main rope the tail rope as they were connected front and rear to the full set parked on the wagon way across the other side. The breaker would then play out the tail rope while his opposite number at the shaft bottom, operating an identical machine, hauled the full set outbye.

Coals were conveyed from the coal face along a belt to a stationary tub at the loading point. Jack Barker, who operated the loader, rested his foot upon a pedal, which he pressed once the tub beneath the loader was full, so that it rolled forward and the next one in line took its place. A double-handled steel tray covered the gap between each tub and caught the spillage, so enabling the belt to run continuously. By pressing a button, Jack could stop the belt at any time. This sometimes became necessary, as, over time, the floor beneath the loader became choked with duff. Then Jack would quickly clear the obstruction with a shovel before restarting the belt.

Tall and lean and rather quiet, Jack was twelve or fifteen years my senior. As a team, we worked well together. My job wasn't all that different to the job I had done at bank. Once the tubs had been filled, I lowered them down the landing and dregged them. When the empty set pulled up to the landing, I switched the ropes, attaching main and tail ropes to the full set, dropping the iron pins into place to secure them to the tubs. After removing all dregs, a signal would be given and the set would then be hauled outbye.

The only other member of the team, even if he was no more than sporadically called into action, was Adam, the breaker on the haulage engine. Adam had been in my mother's class at school, so she told me after I had described him to her. But there were others who passed in and out of the landing in the course of the shift, as their work permitted. Most of them I already knew. Foxy Barlow, who led timber, lived not fifty yards from our house. Freddie Blades had once lived in the same street as me; and Norman Hardy senior had been our next door neighbour in the same street. There wasn't a day went by when Bert, the wagon way man didn't put in an appearance. With his bag of tools slung over his shoulder, Bert patrolled the wagon way, inspecting it for damage, before making the necessary repairs. I quickly became friends with Stan Sinclair, who was always jovial, and a welcome sight whenever he appeared in the flat. Once when the flat was quiet, Stan taught me a drum-playing technique, using two dregs on the side of an empty tub. It was a boon to a fifteen-year-old beginning working life to have so many friendly faces around, and to find acceptance among older men.

Bert was never without a chew in his mouth. On his arrival in the flat, he would stop and survey the scene at the loader before loosing a stream of tobacco juice, which, when it hit the ground, made the stone dust spurt. A lot of men chewed baccy. Dad had his Ladies Twist put on the Store bill and delivered to the house every week with the groceries. Ladies Twist was the best chewing tobacco. The pit canteen also sold Uncle Jeff, which wasn't thought to be as good, but was favoured by men who were unwilling to splash out on Ladies Twist. The tobacco came in lengthy coils, which were then cut into manageable pieces or chews, and kept in a baccy tin. I tried it once. It made my head swim, and although I knew that would pass with use, I refrained from further indulgence mainly because I convinced myself that tobacco would rot the teeth, and I was particular about caring for my teeth. I may have been mistaken about the

The lamp cabin at Murton Colliery.

corrosive effects of tobacco, and it was not an easy decision to make, because I really envied tobacco chewers the enjoyment they derived from their habit. Later, many men began taking snuff. I tried that too, and even bought myself a couple of tins. But I could never take snuff without sneezing, so, in the end, I gave up on that too.

About midway through the shift, Jack and I took time out to eat our sandwiches, holding them by the crusts so as not to blacken them with coal dust. The mice would get the discarded crusts. Water had to be used sparingly, so no more than a couple of mouthfuls would be taken to wash the food down. My sandwiches typically contained fish or meat paste, cheese or dripping, and occasionally beetroot, apple or date. The choice of sandwiches that some men took to work could be unusual, and included Christmas cake between bread. Most men kept their sandwiches in a bait tin to discourage mice, which would make short work of anything wrapped in paper. You might sometimes catch a glimpse of a mouse, or hear one scurrying about in the goaf (worked out area), but generally they remained invisible. It is thought that mice found their way underground hidden in the feed bound for the pit ponies.

Because of our different situations, the power loaders were largely unknown to me. They were faces that I saw at the beginning and end of every shift. I have no doubt that if any one of them were to meet me in the street he would speak in acknowledgement or else give me a nod.

The power loaders were on top money. Working cheek by jowl every day at the coal face, a special bond developed between them. They walked outbye together at the end of every shift, and sat together between the pit props at the shaft bottom, where everyone flopped down while waiting for the onsetter to give the word to ride to bank. A quarter of an hour wait was normal, but it could be longer. The power loaders took part in the repartee during the wait. They also formed what they called a school. Every shift, one of their number would

Hard work at the coal face in a County Durham pit.

bear the responsibility for bringing to work the gob stoppers, with which they filled their mouths while waiting for the cage. Most of them chewed baccy at the coal face, but at the end of the day, they craved sweets. No one in the school ever dared neglect his duty to bring the gob stoppers to work when it became his turn.

Peter Cain was the only power loader I could claim to have been friendly with. Peter was about thirty, easy going, with a ready wit. He was one of those who enlivened matters while we waited for the cage to take us to bank. Foxy Barlow was another; and Foxy sometimes acted as a foil to Peter's ribald humour. But others also contributed to the fun, so that every day at this time the shaft bottom would echo to the sound of men's laughter. As they say in these parts, the crack was good.

I was once sent to the coal face on an errand of some sort. Perhaps one of the men had forgotten his bait, and, as was likely to happen in such an eventuality, food was sent inbye from the pit canteen. The atmosphere was hot and stifling. The men worked naked apart from a pair of pit hoggers, their backs streaked where sweat mingled with dust. The air was thick with coal dust, which glistened like a million tiny gem stones in the glare of the battery lamps. It got everywhere; into the eyes and nostrils and mouth. I was in the midst of it for no more than a moment or two, but before I came away, I was eating the stuff. The men at the coal face were among the highest earners at the pit. Whatever they were paid, it wasn't enough.

Only one disagreeable incident marred my relationship with the men underground. The event had an unfortunate, though entirely unconnected, sequel. One day, I had an altercation with one of the face workers, a man very much older than me, who I thought was a surly individual. He was coming outbye at the end of his shift when I was going in. Maybe I was kicking up too much stone dust, or perhaps I was holding my lamp too high, blinding him. I remain vague about the specific wrong I was accused of, although I have no doubt that I was in the wrong. A mild reproof might have answered, but he was very aggressive in putting me in my place. Fighting underground meant instant dismissal, otherwise I think it might have come to blows. The incident rankled, and I'm afraid that for the rest of the shift and long after I harboured uncharitable thoughts towards the man. I felt only self reproach when, days later, he lost his life in a roof fall.

I was now working all four shifts, first, back, nights and tub loadin'. I found that men commonly hated the tub loadin' shift, when they were obliged to begin work late in the evening and work through the night. One of the reasons, perhaps the main reason, the shift was so detested was because it put such a damper on social life. Visits to pub or club, even the pictures, were curtailed for the duration of the week. I didn't like tub loadin' either, but I preferred it to first shift. From the age of sixteen, when I began to work shifts, I had my own alarm clock. On first shift, it went off at 2.00 am, at which time I got up, got dressed, and went to work underground. Pit work I could cope with quite well; but having to rise from my bed at such an unearthly hour was easily the worst experience of my working life.

The deputy in the district who was on the same shift as me was Mr Laws, the father of Jim Laws, whom I had worked with on the belts. One weekend, without warning, the roof came down over the area of his kist. The place was deserted at the time, so fortunately no one was at risk. Over the weekend, men were put to work clearing away the rubble and transporting it outbye, so that coal production would not be held up. I arrived at the kist on back shift, Monday morning to be met by an astonishing sight. It was like standing in a cathedral. In a monumental feat of labour, hundreds of tons of stone had been removed from the site over the weekend. Where once there had been headroom of not more than seven feet, now the ceiling soared high above like the inside dome of St Paul's.

An engine pulling empty wagons back to Murton after tipping colliery waste at Pesspool, near South Hetton.

You could never afford to be careless in your approach to your work, as danger of one sort or another was an ever-present. I was lucky in that regard. I had one or two inconsequential mishaps, losing a finger nail at one time. On another occasion, I was standing too close to the tail rope when it took the weight of the set, and it swung across to catch me on the back of the head. My pit helmet saved me from possible concussion, but the rope severed the cable of my lamp, plunging me into semi-darkness. For the rest of the shift, I had to rely on the half light shed on the landing by the electric lighting in the vicinity of the main and tail engine. At lowse, I walked outbye by the light of someone else's lamp, hurrying to keep up, fearful of falling behind.

Others weren't as fortunate as me. Sidney Mundin was a likeable twenty something with a tough exterior, who worked in the same district as me. A datal worker, he was inordinately accident prone. Whether it was due to habitual carelessness on his part or because fate had dealt him a poor hand in the matter, Sidney nevertheless seemed always to be busting a finger or suffering some such minor misfortune. A number of us were headed inbye one day when Sidney passed us on his way out. He was travelling under escort, an outsize bandage on his hand, which he held upright. "Finger again, Sidney?" someone inquired. "Aye. Off this time, though," Sidney replied matter-of-factly. I marvelled that he could have been so calm in the circumstances; but Sidney would not have wanted to appear distressed, and, no doubt, was putting on a brave face. He had been inbye for nearly a full shift and his face was streaked with coal dust; but beneath the grime, it was plain to see he was as white as a ghost. Sidney had been docked a finger end that time, missing down to the first joint, and he was eventually able to return to work.

Finally, I was transferred to another district, where I formed a partnership with Norman Thompson, the loader operator on the endless. The endless was the second of the two haulage systems in operation underground, and the name describes the system perfectly. A single cable performed a U turn around a giant wheel at corresponding ends of the pit, inbye and outbye. Tubs, eight in number, called gates or gets, were coupled together and clipped to the endless rope front and rear. The clip was at one end of a length of chain, which had links almost an inch thick. A steel pin connected it to the tub at the other end. When it became attached, the clip imitated the action of a jawbone, biting into the steel cable as it took the weight of the tubs. In this manner, chummins were conveyed to the landing inbye. Once they were filled at the loader, they were shipped outbye in identical fashion. Unlike the main rope of the main and tail system, which pulled the set headlong at an ear-deafening rate, the endless moved at a snail's pace. From one end of the pit to the other, tubs going in both directions would be passing every few seconds.

When the get arrived in the flat, the clip on the leading chummin

Murton Colliery Banner.

had to be loosened and then removed. To loosen it, you had to strike it with an iron bar about the size of a baseball bat. Once both clips had been removed, the get was gradually lowered, sometimes pushed, in the direction of the loader. When the tubs had been filled at the loader, they were let down the landing and dregged, before being clipped to the endless and dispatched outbye. It was essential to observe great care not to leave a finger in the way when affixing the clips. There wasn't a swifter or more efficient amputation once the jaws of an endless clip snapped shut on a finger; and a momentary lapse in concentration cost more than one man a finger end.

At twenty-four, Norman was seven years older than me. Tall and athletic, he was also loquacious, which, because he chewed tobacco constantly, made him liable to swallow the juice, which he did do occasionally. We grew to be great friends while we worked together, and even became related in a way when, years later, Norman's nephew, Brian married my cousin, Anne.

It sometimes happened that when someone at the shaft bottom failed to turn up for his shift, I, or some other young person normally stationed inbye, would be detailed to fill his place. The men worked longer hours at the shaft bottom, for when working inbye, you had to allow an hour each way travelling time. I didn't mind that so much; what I so disliked was the uncertainty of never knowing where I would be working from one day to the next. Still, I wasn't too happy when, after more than two years working inbye, I was assigned to the West Pit shaft bottom to work on a permanent basis. That ended forever my association with the Five Quarter South Drifts.

Chapter Six
A Night at the Club

The Back of the Shaft had a bar extending along the front of the building and a music room to the rear. In the street right of the building, a side door gave access to a small lounge, which wasn't much frequented except by a few men who liked to meet and socialize in a more tranquil pub ambience. They amounted to no more than a dozen at any one time. The lounge also fitted the bill if you liked a drink but didn't want to be seen by too many people. In short, if you were under age.

During 1954, Nicky Jobe was drinking in the lounge of the Back of the Shaft every Friday night, with two or three friends who were mostly former classmates at school. Jackie Duffy was one, and Cliffy might have been another. It wasn't long before Nick talked me into joining them. I took little persuading. It was of small concern to either of us that I was committing and Nick abetting a crime. Everyone in the company except me had passed the age of legal entitlement and could drink in any licensed premises. Being not yet eighteen, and therefore still under age, I was the odd one out.

The only other Friday night regulars were four middle aged men, well known in Murton, who always occupied the same table. During the day, each was engaged in business of one kind or another. Jimmy Anderson owned the paper shop across the way; Mr Nicholson had a grocery business near the top of the Terrace; Mr Salkeld was the brother of a neighbour of ours and the manager of the branch of the Co-op at the end of Barnes Road; and the fourth man was the local undertaker. They were obviously valued customers of long standing, qualifying them for the receipt of a smile from the barmaid, and an exchange of light-hearted chat whenever one or another of their number went to the bar. A bunch of callow youths at a table in their vicinity seemed to cause them no concern. In any case, we were well behaved, and, despite the difference in our ages, we had an interest identical to theirs, desiring nothing more than the enjoyment of a few drinks and some pleasant conversation amongst ourselves.

We drank halves of Scotch, as they did, although I believe everyone in our society eventually became pint drinkers. It didn't take me long to become accustomed to the beer. I had a taste for it from the beginning, and the knowledge that I was engaging in an illegal activity may have given added piquancy to the pleasure. I soon gained

The Travellers Rest – a popular Murton pub for many years

sufficient confidence to approach the bar to order and pay for the drinks whenever it was my round. Nobody queried my age. To the barmaid who filled the glasses, I appeared cloaked with the same invisibility as every other customer she served below the age of fifty. In no time at all, I became perfectly at home in the lounge of the pub, when Friday night was an occasion much anticipated and enjoyed.

Dad never drank in the Back of the Shaft. At weekends, he gave his custom to the Village Inn, the Knaresborough or the Demi Club, and twice during the week he took my mother to the pictures. Dad was virtually a stranger to the Miners' Hall opposite; but some function or other drew him there one night. By a luckless circumstance of fate, mine not his, it was a Friday night. A break in the programme of events found Dad and two of his friends feeling dry. The Back of the Shaft being conveniently close by provided the ideal opportunity for the three of them to take a few minutes break to assuage their thirst.

Typical drinkers from the 1950s.

When Dad pushed open the door of the lounge, the first person he saw was me, relaxing in accustomed style, beer glass in hand. Caught completely off guard, I reacted instinctively. As Dad and his friends crowded around the little bar, I made a bolt for the door and vanished into the night. I guessed that Dad would have been none too pleased about my drinking while under age. Back home, when at last I had to face him, he merely asked me where I had disappeared to.

Kiddo was forever asking me to spend a night in his neck of the woods. It seemed only fair since Kiddo came to Murton every once in a while. Seeing as he lived no more than five miles away, and the bus service was a good and reliable one, I really had no excuse to fall back on. Even if I were to miss the last bus home, it wasn't all that much of a walk. So, in the end, I agreed. Nick knew Kiddo through me and he promised to come too. We set a Friday night apart, and for the first time for both of us, we went out of the place to find our pleasure.

Kiddo being a few weeks younger than me, was also under age; but I knew that he liked a drink. Unlike me, he didn't have a regular pub he could call his local. He met us off the bus about sevenish, when the three of us directed our steps to the Black Horse, a William Deuchar house on the corner of a minor junction. It was a bright, cheery looking establishment, very inviting to three fledgling imbibers, for whom pub life was still a novel experience.

Nicky Jobe with friend.

Passing through the swing door, we took a few steps inside. It was early. Two men were parleying at the far end of the bar.

A sign behind the bar proclaimed the legend: Stan and Brenda Welcome You to the Black Horse. A tall man, forty something, with a crew cut, was polishing a glass while taking a perfunctory interest in the small talk of the other two. Seeing us, he put the glass down and came over to our end of the bar

"Three pints," Nick said.

This must have been Stan, and he wasn't very welcoming.

"You eighteen?" he shot at Kiddo.

"That's right," Kiddo lied.

"You sure?"

Kiddo didn't bat an eye. "As a matter of fact, I was eighteen on Tuesday."

"Happy birthday," said Stan sarcastically, "You don't look eighteen."

Kiddo pretended to be offended. "Well, Aa can't help that."

The Knaresboro Hotel – now a private residence.

Stan reached for a pint glass. I breathed an inward sigh of relief. It looked like we had gotten away with it. Stan gave Nick no more than a cursory glance. Nick was a big lad, with a shock of strong brown hair that even then was streaked with grey. He always looked his age and could pass for older. As Stan pulled the first pint, he eyed me suspiciously. "And you. How old are you?"

"Nineteen," I said, trying to appear unruffled. All under age drinkers when asked said they were eighteen. I thought I might sound more convincing if I said nineteen. Stan raised an eyebrow. "Just gone," I hastily added. I was adding about sixteen months to my actual age.

"And I'm a hundred and two," Stan said. He nevertheless filled the remaining glasses and took the money.

We went and sat by the window. Kiddo lit a cigarette before downing about a third of his pint. Nick and I took it a bit slower. I surveyed the surroundings. The pub was like many others that were built in the nineteenth century to accommodate a growing mining population. No one would have called it opulent; more like snug. The table we sat at was like all the others, heavy, ornate iron frame with a thick, hardwood top, chamfered around the edges. Mirrors bearing commercials for various drinks adorned the walls of the room. Perched massively on a shelf above the bar was a row of hogsheads. A lot of Victoriana was rooted out of public houses a couple of decades later, when a number of quaint old pubs were turned into trendy wine bars. But it was mostly towns like Sunderland that were affected.

Nick played with a beer mat, flipping it over between his fingers, in pensive mood. After a while, he told us of an idea he had for a short story. It concerned a clandestine relationship between a man and a woman who frequented the same pub separately and at different times, and who left messages for one another on the underside of beer mats. I thought he had the germ of a good story, but although I didn't say so, it seemed to me the device entailed a certain risk. Someone else might sit at the table in the meantime and discover the message. Or the barman might exchange the beer mats for new ones. But I wasn't about to put a damper on Nick's idea. In any case, he probably would have realized the difficulty and devised a way round it.

We were about ready for a second pint when a door behind the bar opened and a blonde woman entered, about forty, plain looking and a touch over made up. This must have been Brenda. With barely a glance in our direction, Brenda immediately got into discussion with the two men at the other end of the bar, who were obviously regulars. Every few seconds, she would laugh aloud in rather vulgar fashion at something one of them said. I got up to get the drinks in. "Just get halves. We'll move on after this," Kiddo said. Brenda was happily chatting away but left off in order to serve me. Heedless of Kiddo's advice, I ordered pints. It simplified matters. Brenda took the money, thanked me and gave me my change, before returning to take up where she had left off in her small talk with the two regulars.

We were debating where to go next when Kiddo suggested the club further down the street. At that time, neither Nick nor myself had ever been in a working men's club, and we expressed some doubt as to whether they would let us in. Kiddo, who had never set foot in one either, was more sanguine. He swore he knew of lads of his own age who were regularly admitted. We supped off and left, without the benefit of a goodbye from either Stan or Brenda.

Three minutes walk brought us to the club, an undistinguished brick building of 1930s era, a few yards back from the main street. Inside, an elderly man in a three piece suit sat at a table smoking a pipe. The doorman. He looked up as we came in and ran an eye over the three of us as we stood gazing around self consciously.

"Are you lads members?" he inquired, in a tone not unfriendly.

We shook our heads.

"Come from out of the place?"

We nodded.

"Affiliated?"

Kiddo looked at me and then at Nick. "What's that?"

The old gentleman narrowed his eyes and peered intently at the three of us. "You are all over the age of eighteen, Aa suppose?"

We nodded vigorously.

He puffed on his pipe before reaching for a pen. Turning to a big man who was standing behind him intently studying a notice board, he said, "Gordon, sign these lads in. Mind you" – he pointed the pen at us – "Behave yourselves. Let's have no carryin' on." Kiddo and I made appropriate noises. Nick said, "All we want is to have a quiet drink and to enjoy the entertainment."

"That's all right, then,"

Every club had a committee and here are the committee men of the Temperance and Literary Institute, 1948. Back row: M. Thompson, W. Tilly, T, Miller, J. Routledge, D. Turner, W. Curtis, W. Cook, G. Waddell. Front: W. Anderson, J, Miller (Secretary), W. Treweeke, J.H. Clabburn (Treasurer) and W. Collins. Being Temperance meant it was a club that didn't sell beer – a situation that was rectified when it became the Ex-Servicemen's Club.

said the old man, nodding with satisfaction. "They don't look like troublemakers, do they, Gordon?"

Gordon gave us a wink before obligingly appending his signature to the relevant forms. We signed our names, recording our place of origin as Murton, and laid out the few coppers according to the rule, after which we pocketed the receipts and thanked them both. "Told you we'd get in," Kiddo said under his breath as we walked away. Behind us, the door opened and two smartly dressed men and a glamorous looking woman entered.

"Gordon, tell Clem the concert party's arrived," said the old man.

The murmur of many voices, intermittently punctuated by hearty outbursts of laughter, greeted the three of us as we entered the great rectangle of a concert room and paused at the door. Formica topped tables, piled with glasses, crowded the floor from end to end, except for the area around a busy bar. Diametrically across from the bar, the room boasted a fair sized stage with curtains on three sides. I brightened at the promise of entertainment. It had come as a surprise when I learned that the back room of the Back of the Shaft had a piano and drum kit.

It was about four fifths full when we arrived. There weren't too many young people present, but that didn't put us off. Kiddo pointed to what appeared to be a vacant table against the wall on the far side of the room, so the three of us weaved our way across. As we took our seats, people on a nearby table nodded a friendly greeting. A woman smiled and asked me if it was our first time in the concert room on a Friday night. I said it was, without troubling to explain that two of us were from out of the place. She said she thought so because she hadn't seen us before and didn't think we were part of the usual Friday night crowd. It crossed my mind that she might have been hinting that we seemed under age, but she appeared genuine and I dismissed the thought.

Waitresses in aprons were moving from table to table taking orders. Kiddo caught the eye of one and ordered three pints of Fed best. "Three pints of best." The waitress repeated the order so she wouldn't forget it. After filling her tray with empties, she called over her shoulder "Be right back, pet." I leant back contentedly and relaxed against the plush upholstery. These people could teach Stan and Brenda a thing or two about hospitality, I thought to myself.

The waitress soon returned with the order, which Kiddo paid for. Downing three or four mouthfuls of the beer, he set his glass down and sat back and lit a cigarette. Neither Nick nor I smoked, which put us very much in a minority here. A fog of cigarette smoke hung over the scene. I took a long draught of the beer. Replacing the glass on the table, I glanced at the others. "Good pint," Nick said, licking his lips. I nodded in agreement.

A man in his forties looking ridiculous in a Tony Curtis haircut appeared at the table. "Double numbers, lads? Only six left." We got him to explain. You picked two of a limited number from the card,

One of Murton's clubs – The Victoria or 'The Big Club'.

and if those two numbers were drawn, you won the money prize. We studied his card and made our selection, before forking out the money. A roll of drums followed by a clash of symbols drew our attention to the stage. A dapper little man in a red bow tie that might at any other time have looked incongruous and marked him down as an oddball but which seemed to suit the present occasion well enough was preparing to make an announcement.

"Ladies and gentlemen." He began, before stopping to tap the mike and blow into it a few times. "Clem speaking, 1, 2, 3," he said, his voice resonating throughout the room. Satisfied that the mike was in working order, he continued. "Ladies and gentlemen, you'll be pleased to hear that the concert party has arrived, and the entertainment will begin in a few minutes." Apparently, the concert party had lost its way, and there had been some doubt whether it would appear or not.

A concert party would comprise three or four artists, whose usual programme consisted of a number of songs performed as solos, but also in various plural combinations. This type of club entertainment had virtually disappeared by the end of the decade. Electric guitar groups came to dominate the club scene from about 1960, and I think it was about then that the cover charge was introduced. Later, balladeers gained in popularity with club audiences. This must have coincided with one of Frank Sinatra's comebacks; so a lengthy period ensued when the guitar groups were superseded by an epidemic of Sinatra and Tony Bennett imitators.

Perhaps ten minutes elapsed before a ripple of applause caused us to focus our attention once more on the stage. The young woman we had seen entering the club after us was standing before the mike, wearing an off-the-shoulder, ankle length green gown and a confident smile. Clem, the MC, reached for the mike. "Ladies and gentlemen," his voice boomed, "can I have your attention, please!" The buzz of conversation gradually tailed off. People were going "Shush!" to those of their neighbours who seemed heedless of the need for quiet. Clem waited until he had everyone's attention. "Ladies and gentlemen, to get the night's entertainment under way, let's have the best or order and a big round of applause for Miss Eleanor Burns!" Clem gave the last three words an extra accentuation. He stood for a moment leading what was no more than polite applause; for the soloist was unknown to the audience and no one knew if she was any good.

Club entertainment in the 1950s – this is believed to be in the Demi Club.

Turning to the accompanist on the organ, Miss Burns gave him a nod, whereupon he played a few introductory bars of the song she had chosen to perform. Clem left the stage, and soon a hush descended upon the room as the pure notes of Franz Lehar's Vilia filled the air. Vilia was in the repertoire of every soprano who ever graced the stage of a working men's club. So familiar was it, that many of the women and not a few of the men began to join in. Still, Miss Eleanor Burns did have a beautiful voice. During the ovation at the conclusion of the number, Nick passed some remark I couldn't quite catch. Two men on the next table, who had hardly noticed us before, flashed Nick an unfriendly look. Perhaps they imagined that he had made some negative comment about Miss Burns' performance. They seemed to be daring him to repeat it. Maybe they thought that, being so young, we would not appreciate anything classical. Like me, Nick liked most kinds of music. He accordingly lavished a few words of praise on Miss Burns' performance, as did I. Kiddo also indicated appreciation, feigned in his case, I fancied. That evidently pleased the two music lovers.

"Falling in love with love," Eleanor trilled, already into her next number. I was transported by the clear, bell-like tones of her voice and applauded wildly at the end, as, indeed, did everyone present. They were an appreciative audience.

Clem came to the front of the stage to take the mike from Eleanor's hand, and stood waiting for the applause to die down. Making Eleanor a chivalrous gesture, he bellowed into the mike, "How was that, then, eh?" Clem paused before making another chivalrous gesture. "A lovely rendition of a lovely song. Ladies and gentlemen, put your hands together for that wonderful songstress, the pride of Jarra, Miss Eleanor Burns!" Eleanor stood with a smile on her countenance and graciously accepted the applause, which broke out again, and even increased a decibel, if I know anything about decibels.

There followed a brief interlude. Nick got the drinks in, so I emptied my glass. The man with the Tony Curtis haircut came round again.

"Any double numbers, lads?"

"We've already got them," I reminded him.

"That was the last card. This is a new one."

"What won the last time?" said Kiddo.

"Er – two and sixteen. It was broadcast over the mike." He indicated a huge man about four tables away. "Large area won it." He held the new card out for us to see. A few numbers were gone but most were unclaimed. We each of us selected fresh numbers and he eliminated them from among the options, pencilling our names against them on the card. Moving on to the table left of ours, he directed a hopeful look at the middle aged couple sitting there, but the man waved him away. They were having some sort of a disagreement, a domestic. "I brought you here, didn't I?" the man was heard to say. Looking far from happy, the woman had set her back to him and remained tight-lipped.

We kept our ears pricked for the next few minutes in case one of us had the winning combination. Kiddo's numbers came up, so he ordered an extra round of drinks. Childlike, he beamed his delight at winning the draw. A drum roll prefaced the appearance of one of the men from the concert party, who bounded on stage flashing a toothy smile, before being introduced as Bobby Breeze. Bobby was rigged out in a striped blazer of a kind

Another of Murton's Clubs – The Officials' Club.

no one would have dared wear on the street, not for a month's wages. Like Clem, he sported a bow tie, white with green spots in Bobby's case. A Moe Howerd haircut completed the picture. Everything about him said comedian.

Sure enough, Bobby kicked off by telling a string of jokes, which went down well, bringing guffaws of laughter from the men while the women shrieked helplessly, especially at the risqué jokes. Then, in a complete change of character, Bobby surprised everybody by following up with a song delivered in a very good bass baritone voice. These club artists were really good, I thought to myself. Continuing in serious vein, Bobby brought the house down with his next number, Old Man River, which he performed with every dramatic gesture and intonation you could almost imagine him hefting bales of cotton on the Mississippi. Finishing the number on an emotional high, Bobby acknowledged the applause by taking a succession of bows before leaving the stage. It was my round and Nick was low in the glass, so I beckoned the waitress and ordered three pints. Time was passing very pleasantly. I glanced at my watch. Ten past nine already.

Five minutes elapsed before Clem reappeared to introduce Ron McGuin, who opened with a rendition of River of No Return, a Tennessee Ernie number. He was very like him. There was the same rich, baritonal quality to Ron's voice. He even managed to look like Tennessee Ernie. The feuding couple to our left were proving a distraction, but were shushed into silence by those nearby. I felt nervous, seated next to them. Ron reprised with Give Me Your Word, Tennessee Ernie's biggest hit. I drifted into a reverie, then found myself observing the barmaids, busily filling trays of pint glasses at the bar. Those women certainly earned their money. "Give me your word you'll feel the same as I," Ron intoned. The song gave rise to a warm, euphoric feeling, although I imagine the drink contributed something to the mood. One of the men to our right turned to mouth the words, "Very good," indicating Ron. Soundlessly, Nick and I both agreed. Kiddo was reclining with his head back, blowing smoke rings. His mind seemed to be elsewhere, but he might have been listening. Matters were becoming heated at the next table.

"You take me for granted."

"Rubbish!"

"Yes, you do."

"No, Aa don't."

"Do."

"Don't."

"Our love will never die," Ron crooned into the mike.

Ron finished the number to a richly deserved ovation. He bowed his thanks and left the stage. Disapproving looks were being cast at the couple next to me, who now had fallen silent and were sulking.

Inside the Big Club in the 1950s.

Clem was on stage, taking charge of the mike. "Thank you, Ron," he trumpeted. "Wasn't that sensational, ladies and gentlemen? Close your eyes and its Tennessee Ernie. Show your appreciation for Ron, everybody." Clem stood acclaiming the performance. He allowed the applause to die down before clearing his throat. "Ladies and gentlemen, there will now be a short intermission while Harry and Glen go round with the letter draw." Clem indicated two men, one on either side of the room, who were at that moment moving from table to table, seeking punters. "It'll be drawn Sunday night, ladies and gentlemen," said Clem. "Just to remind you, the jackpot now stands at sixty pounds. I thank you."

We declined to buy into the letter draw as we wouldn't be present on Sunday night when it was to be drawn. Kiddo summoned the waitress and ordered another round of Fed best. The beer was going down well. Tony Curtis was back. "Only four numbers left, lads. D'ye want them?" Since we had won the draw once, we felt almost duty bound to oblige him. "Go on, we'll have them," I said, fishing for the money in my pocket. We must have been his best customers. We listened for the announcement of the draw, but we were out of luck this time.

The short intermission stretched to half an hour, before Ron was back on stage with Miss Eleanor Burns, when they got the second half of the show off to a start with the duet, Ah Sweet Mystery of Life. They followed this with Only Make Believe and Why Do I Love You from Showboat, Eleanor winsome as the Riverboat captain's daughter, and Ron cutting a dashing figure as Gaylord Ravenal. I reached for my glass, only to find another resting alongside it, full. Emptying the first glass, I pushed it to the middle of the table for the glass collector to pick up, before setting the full one in its place. The singer-comedian, Bobby Breeze, now in the role of serious bass baritone, came to the mike and sang a solo. Then Eleanor returned to sing a solo, and then Ron. Finally, all three artists got together as a trio for a short medley of songs in a smash hit finale. As the performers took their final bows, Nick and I were on our feet applauding wildly. Kiddo was contemplating his pint, in a world of his own. Kiddo was behaving strangely, slurring his words.

"Want any football teams, you lads?"

It was Harry, who, a short time before, had been the vendor for the letter draw. "Aa've got Fulham and Bristol Rovers left." He eyed us eagerly, card and pen in hand. I took Bristol Rovers and Nick took Fulham. That filled Harry's card so he went away happy.

Murton people enjoying themselves in the Ex-Servicemen's Club.

The members of the concert party were taking their leave, and in last minute conversation with Clem, who, no doubt, would have been promising them a return booking. A glance at my watch told me that three hours had passed since Gordon signed us in; it seemed like thirty minutes. I felt a tinge of disappointment that the night was drawing to a close. Dreamily, I marvelled at the relative nature of time. If I had suffered toothache for three hours it would have seemed like an eternity. I gazed out of a warm haze at Nick, who was playing with beer mats again, and wondered if I sounded as silly as Kiddo. I heard the words, "Last orders, please!" and was about to flag a waitress when Nick suggested we leave so as not to miss the last bus home.

Rising, we wished everyone around us a good night. To get to the exit, I found myself navigating an obstacle course, dodging bodies, and tables laden with drinks. Everything and everyone seemed to be swimming in a vortex. Faces appeared before me and then vanished. Voices were all around. "Goodnight." "Will we see you next week, then?" "Safe journey." Someone waved a book of tickets. "Jolly Boys Raffle, anybody?" I was a mite unsteady on my feet; nevertheless, I managed to lurch to the exit without upsetting anybody's drink. Compared to Kiddo, I was a rock. Nick had to hold him up at one stage.

We struck out along the street in the direction of the bus stop, Nick as sober as a judge, me rather less so; but the Banana Kid was really feeling the effects of the drink. It was a crisp autumn night, not at all bad for that time of year. The cool night air was in distinct contrast to the warm atmosphere of the club that had enveloped us for the past hours. As we walked, Kiddo kept bumping into Nick and me. The path alongside the road must have been four feet wide and he was having trouble remaining on it. The two of us were a bit concerned about Kiddo finding his way home alright, so we agreed to see him to the door of his house even if it meant missing the last bus back to Murton. Our difficulty was solved by a chance encounter with two youths, one of whom lived in the same street as Kiddo, and who consented to escort him home. We managed to catch the bus alright, but I almost wish we had set off to walk back. It was the last bus of the night, and the way ahead spanned three miles of open country without a solitary stop. The driver, his shift near completion and anxious to be home, consequently tore off at breakneck speed, throwing the dozen or so passengers into confusion at every twist of the road. I got off a stop before Nick, who was living at Cornwall at the time. After that, what was left of the night was pretty much of a blank, except for the memory of a momentary technological hitch in getting my front door key to fit the lock.

I rose late the next morning feeling nauseous. A blacksmith was shoeing a horse inside my head. I thought if I splashed my face liberally with cold water it might help. It didn't. I managed to force down some breakfast cereal and half a cup of tea, hoping that my mother would not pass comment on my sudden loss of appetite. I was glad that it was mid morning and that bacon and eggs was no longer a breakfast option. I couldn't have faced that. Mam said nothing, but her silence was more eloquent than words. I knew that she knew what ailed me; I also knew that I could expect no sympathy from that quarter.

Straight after breakfast, I went for a walk. I thought it better to suffer alone and outdoors than remain conspicuously out of sorts indoors. I had about an hour to kill before I was due to leave for Sunderland. I dearly wanted to give the pictures a miss, but I had promised to meet Kiddo, and I was determined not to disappoint him. I expected Kiddo to be on the bus when I boarded at the Police Station, but he was nowhere to be seen. Nor was he waiting for me in Park Lane. I hung around until the next number 21 pulled in, but still no Kiddo. Another twenty minutes elapsed, when it became clear that he was not going to put in an appearance that day; so I got on the bus for the return journey, cursing Kiddo all the way home. I guessed he was hung over after the previous night's carousing. But so was I. If I could make the effort to keep our appointment, why couldn't he, I kept telling myself.

Alighting from the bus at the Colliery Inn, I went for a walk over the park in the hope that the fresh air would dispel any remaining fuzziness from my head. While strolling in the park, I ran into Robert Cairns and Freddie Blades, who both worked in the South Drifts, and the three of us had a game of bowls. As the day wore on, I felt a good deal better. After tea, I spent some time in my room, before going out to meet Nick and Cliffy, when we went to the Empire to see Bad Day at Black Rock.

Murton Colliery Welfare Park – a good place to walk off a hang-over.

Chapter Seven
Shall We Dance?

Kiddo approached me one day in a flush of excitement beseeching me to go with him to the Saturday night dance at Easington, where, he assured me, the girls were just waiting to be swept off their feet. I had not attended a dance since I left school. Moreover, girls in their late teens were mature years away from when they were the objects of juvenile crushes, and knowing Kiddo's proneness to exaggeration, I expressed some doubt as to the truth of what he claimed.

"Are you kidd'n'?" Kiddo was incredulous. "At Easington? The Hunchback of Notre Dame could 'ave 'is pick!"

This was no reflection of the fair sex of Easington, for people came from miles around to attend Saturday night dances.

Before it became the fashion to dance more or less alone, in a spontaneous manner, people used to dance with partners of the opposite sex; and there were certain dance techniques that had to be learnt. I acquired a familiarity with dances like the Dashing White Sergeant and the Boston Two Step while still at school, when revelling in social evenings in St Joseph's church hall; but, after leaving school, I soon forgot them. Moreover, the modern form of dancing differed radically from these exuberant old time numbers. Whereas I was taught to waltz in a way that involved bouncing on the balls of the feet while counting 1, 2, 3 in time to the music, the modern waltz seemed to be more of a low key adaptation.

Easington wasn't the only village that held a Saturday night dance, although there tended to be a vogue in popularity which shifted from one place to the next. Easington was currently the in place. For a long time, a weekly dance was conducted at a parish hall in South Hetton. Later in the decade, following a slump in the popularity of snooker, the Billiard Hall in Murton was turned into a dance hall by a local entrepreneur known only as Johnny; by which cognomen his identity was sufficiently established beyond the confines of Murton even. For a time, Murton became the best attended Saturday night venue for dancing. Murton had a regular late night bus service, and a bus stop directly outside the dance hall.

Easington dance hall was located at the Colliery, about a mile east of Easington Village, where it occupied the first floor of the Welfare Hall. It was noted for its sprung floor, which made dancing more pleasurable and was kind on the feet. Saturday night dances,

A contemporary advert for dance lessons.

wherever they were held, were always well attended. For local youth, it was the place to be and to be seen; even though there were those who seldom took to the floor and some not at all. Friends of the same sex, when they were not gracing the dance floor, customarily wandered about the hall, elbowing their way through the crowd, or else, convened in small knots, and, in raised voices, endeavoured to talk above the brassy notes of the live orchestra.

Dances were always something of a fashion show, particularly for the male of the species, and especially where hair was concerned. Smart young men exulted in their Tony Curtis and DA haircuts; although there were those who, lagging behind in the fashion, were loathe to forsake the short-back-and-sides look, which was the only hairstyle favoured by their fathers. Whatever the style, hair was every youth's pride and joy, and premature baldness was a catastrophe not to be contemplated. Not even Yul Brynner, who rose to cinematic prominence about this time, could persuade young men to eschew hair, and it would be decades before the shaved head look caught on. In the 1950s, for boys no less than for girls, it was simply unthinkable to be without a well groomed head of hair. And no young man went anywhere without his comb, which was usually kept in the breast pocket of his jacket.

Pony tails were favoured by some girls, although short cropped hair was becoming fashionable. When it became really short, it tended to blur the distinction between the sexes; for until then long hair was equated with girls and short hair with boys. The fashion for shoulder-length hair among young men, which further blurred if it did not reverse the trend, was still some years off. Girls wore a la mode spread out dresses reinforced by layers of net petticoats, and commonly enhanced their appearance by applying lipstick and rouge, before smothering the result in powder.

I spied Kiddo in the crush at the top of the stairs. He had bussed through from his own locality and arrived about the same time as me. The two of us advertised our presence by going walkabout, jostling in and out of the throng until we had completed a full circuit of the dance hall, without, I might add, making any huge impression on the females present beyond evoking the odd, perfunctory glance. Beneath where the band was rendering its version of the Tennessee Waltz, I got into discussion with George Dobson, a neighbourhood friend, who was one of numerous Murtonians present. But we were barely able to make ourselves heard for the trumpet solo, and grew tired of shouting "What did you say?" at one another. When I turned around, Kiddo had vanished.

Hanging about on the fringe of the ballroom, I cast an eye over the sea of swirling figures, taking note of the manoeuvres. Some of the lads appeared stiff. I supposed them to be beginners like me and was heartened by the thought. I

Handsome hair
when you check Dry Scalp

Let's face it—healthy hair is handsome hair. Oil-starved roots and Dry Scalp just won't let your hair have that neat and natural, well-groomed look.

A few drops of 'Vaseline' Brand Hair Tonic, massaged gently into the scalp each morning, will check Dry Scalp, supplement the natural scalp oils and promote healthy, neat, and handsome hair.

Why not let 'Vaseline' Hair Tonic help *your* hair to be its natural good-looking self? Buy a bottle today.

Dry, scruffy hair? Hair that is hard to manage? Your trouble is probably Dry Scalp. Check Dry Scalp by massaging daily with 'Vaseline' Hair Tonic.

Just twenty seconds every morning and see the difference! 'Vaseline' Hair Tonic supplements the natural scalp oils, keeps hair *naturally* handsome all day.

Vaseline* HAIR TONIC
The dressing that checks Dry Scalp

'Vaseline' is the registered trade mark of the Chesebrough Mfg. Co. Ltd.   6001-15

Every youth's pride and joy. An advert for well groomed hair.

reckoned I could give the modern waltz a go (it wasn't as easy as it looked, I later discovered) but other dances appeared to require greater proficiency. I had no intention of attempting the foxtrot, which everyone, even accomplished dancers, allowed was difficult.

Presently, I found the courage to present myself to a girl in a smart yellow dress, who was one of a group of four girls all about the same age. She was partly detached from the others, which was the reason I fixed on her. "Excuse me, but would you like to dance?" I inquired with exaggerated politeness. I believe I only just prevented myself from making a little bow. She turned her face to mine, then to her companions, who were all smirking in an infantile manner as though they had just noticed that I had two heads, before all four collapsed into peals of laughter.

I walked away crestfallen; but, analysing the incident, I soon realized where I had gone wrong. I was affecting to be too gentlemanlike, too much of a Jane Austen gallant. This wasn't the debutante's ball, I told myself. These were ordinary, working class girls, and their partners were mostly young miners, like myself. I would have wagered any sum of money there wasn't a Rupert or a Tarquin in the building. Be respectful, that's alright, I thought, giving myself a mental kick up the backside, but be casual, and drop the airs and graces.

I awaited my next opportunity, before making a casual approach to a tall, dark haired girl, who was also one of a group. "Care to dance?" I drawled in an off-hand manner. She hesitated, seeming not unwilling, I thought, when suddenly a stocky youth with greasy black hair and a centre parting bounded into view and grabbed her by the wrist. "Hey, Val, let's go, eh!" he exclaimed, as he hauled her headlong onto the dance floor. Val tossed her head and laughed her pleasure.

They capered around the floor together, leaving me looking on. In my judgement, a prejudiced one possibly, he was a lousy dancer; but the girl seemed blissful in his arms. The experience gave me further pause for thought. Here was I striving to impress the girls by giving a poor imitation, first of Michael Wilding then of Randolph Scott, when all along it was Marlon Brando who was inhabiting their dreams. Here, I thought, was the proof of Kiddo's claim. Find the right modus operandi – become appealingly uncouth – and the girls really could be swept off their feet.

Kiddo reappeared as I was taking stock of the situation. "Any luck?" he queried. "Nah." I shrugged my shoulders nonchalantly as if to say I haven't really made much of an effort as I'm not all that interested. "How about you?" Kiddo made a similar gesture of indifference. "Not really bothered."

I refrained from observing that Kiddo seemed distinctly disinclined to put to the proof his own theory, by which artifice he had sought to get me here in the first place.

Dwelling on my recent disappointments, my thoughts ran on as I got to rehearsing what I would say and how I would present myself whenever the next

A dance hall scene from around the late 1950s.

opportunity occurred. I was trying not to listen to Kiddo, who was rambling on about one thing or another, interrupting my train of thought. "Have you seen the Caine Mutiny, yet? Brilliant! Humphrey Bogart's a mental case. He's captain of this boat, see, well a ship, and he goes loopy in the middle of a typhoon. Or it might have been a hurricane." I was beginning to get a little annoyed with Kiddo.

A considerable surge in activity immediately focussed my attention. Multitudes were heading for the dance floor, the reason, I learned, was that the band dance was about to commence. Evidently, the band dance was awaited with eagerness by dancers and clodhoppers alike. In the first place, the dance steps were simplicity itself, as I discerned while watching the dance in progress. You took two steps in then two steps out before shuffling around in a circle; then two steps in, two steps out and two steps to the side, at which point you exchanged partners. Orang-utans could be taught it. Then, as you progressed from one partner to the next, you got to dance, however briefly, with practically every girl in the place. Obtaining a partner seemed to present no difficulty at all, for no girl would wish to be left conspicuously solitary when almost everyone else was on the floor. In fact, it appeared that all you had to do was stroll onto the dance floor and eventually you would be paired off with someone. Unfortunately, once paired off and into your step, you were given time to utter no more than a pleasantry or two before moving on to the next partner. By the end of the dance, you had said "Hello. Where are you from?" to a hundred girls, but hardly anything else. Nonetheless, after observing the often ungainly efforts of many on the floor, I resolved to make an attempt at it the next time around.

Some twenty or so minutes elapsed after the band dance before I decided to try my luck again. The orchestra was about to play a modern waltz. I stalked a redhead in a green chequered dress, hoping she would stand still long enough for me to ask her to dance. I wanted to catch her on her own, but pretty soon she joined a little circle of friends. I hung around in their vicinity, waiting for them to fall silent. It seemed they never would. The orchestra struck up a few introductory notes of the waltz, and I began to grow impatient. Finally a lull in the conversation gave me my opportunity. Emboldened, I drew near, and, taking a leaf out of the book of my youthful mentor, seized her wrist. She turned towards me, engagingly fresh faced and slightly freckled. "How about a whirl around the floor then, Red?" I said, indicating the dance floor with an insouciant inclination of the head, and hoping I came across like the youth with the centre parting and the greasy black hair. "Well –" she began. One of her girl friends gave her a nudge. "Go on, Terry, we won't mind." Terry smiled agreeably. "Alright, then." Elated by my success, I turned smartly about, tripped over my own feet and fell flat on my face.

For the second time that night I brought the house down in side splitting fashion. To be fair, one of the girls asked me if I was alright, and Terry was covering her mouth with her hand, trying not to laugh. Mortified, I retreated to where Billy Bell and George "Ikey" Reah were propping up the back wall of the building. They hadn't witnessed my faux pas, and, eventually, I got into conversation with them. Here I remained in ignominious seclusion. I even let a band dance go by, for I couldn't face the likelihood of encountering Terry or any of her friends on the dance floor; and I felt sure that, at this very moment, I was being pointed out by numerous persons, including every girl in the hall, as the clumsy lout who had toppled face down at the feet of a party of girls. Had I been twenty years older, the incident might have been laughed off; as it was, it had assumed the magnitude of an unmitigated disaster.

After a while, I went looking for Kiddo, who had disappeared again. By the end of the night, I was still looking for him. I blamed Kiddo when I missed the last bus and had to get home by

Easington Welfare Hall, a popular venue for dances.
Above: The old Hall before a fire in the 1930s.
Below: A more recent photograph.

Shanks' pony. This was made bearable by the company of Maurice Brewster and Billy Gray, who also had missed the last bus home. However, before we had covered the first quarter mile, I realized that their company was a mixed blessing. Maurice was six feet four and Billy only marginally shy of that, and as I was, at most, five feet nine, for the six mile hike back to Murton I was having to take two strides to their one.

The following afternoon, I went with Cliffy to Brunini's ice cream shop, where we occupied a booth in the back room, and where, shortly, we were joined by Nick. It was customary for young people to pass away an hour on a Sunday afternoon in either

Pioli's on the Terrace or Brunini's by the High House. Mr Brunini got a decent trade out of us. If everybody bought say, an iced drink to begin with, then, maybe later, a special, I imagine that would have been more than enough to keep him happy.

On this particular Sunday, I couldn't help feeling that I was being observed, and I very easily convinced myself that it was on account of my humiliating experience of the night before. Every time someone glanced in my direction, I imagined the incident was being recounted, and possibly embellished, for the benefit of those who had not been present. Every time a girl laughed aloud, I required no further proof that she was laughing at me. The experience made me restive, and left me wondering if my paranoia was apparent to my companions. Thus it was a relief when we quit the ice cream parlour to go for a walk over the park.

By the time we had walked up to the entrance gates of the park and down the long drive past St Joseph's school field and the Colliery Welfare sports fields on the one side, and, on the other, the cemetery and allotments, we had covered not much short of a mile. It was possible to arrive at the park by a route which went past the blacksmith's shop, but the distance was hardly less. A leisurely promenade around several of the tree-lined avenues that criss-crossed the park, then a return to our starting point outside Brunini's, added up to a three mile walk. It was then tea time. Cliffy lived close by, but Nick and I still had another mile ahead of us before arriving home.

As a trio, we were fond of walking, a spare time occupation that many in Murton found agreeable. Together, we once walked to Easington Lane, along the B1285 out of Murton, a road that wound and dipped an uneven course before emerging at the main street of the neighbouring pit village, where we had a few drinks in the club on the corner before walking home. On another occasion, after Cliffy remarked that a Mario Lanza picture was being screened at the Princess in Dawdon, near Seaham, the three of us set off to walk, passing through historic Dalton-le-Dale and along the scenic Harbour Road, returning by the same route after the show.

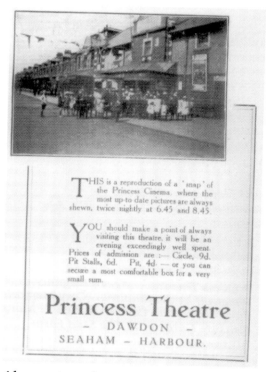

Above: An advert for the Princess in Dawdon.

Left: The walk home through Dalton-le-Dale.

I didn't see much of Kiddo after the fiasco at Easington, which was followed, in my case, by a return to the accustomed routine of Saturday night attendance at the pictures. Soon Thornley took the place of Easington as the in place for Saturday night dances. I was busy at the West Pit shaft bottom at the time, working marras with Abert Swan, with whom I was also in regular association away from work. Albert was always fairly nifty on his feet. He was keen to see what the new dance venue at Thornley was like, and wanted me to go with him. I was of a mind not to go. It can be pretty devastating at eighteen knowing you have less sex appeal than the Hunchback of Notre Dame. I had to be persuaded. Finally, I was, and agreed to tag along with Albert that coming Saturday.

Although Thornley was the birthplace of my paternal grandmother, I had never once ventured there. Neither, it might reasonably have been supposed, had anyone else in Murton, until the Saturday night dance drew people there. Previously, nobody ever had any reason to visit the place. Not that Thornley was of a character and reputation likely to deter visits – for all we knew it might have been the very model of a thriving and well-ordered community – but because it was thought to be too remote. Thornley was the end of the line for the Northern bus company, the opposite terminus being Sunderland. And Thornley was about the same distance from Murton as Sunderland in the other direction, too far to walk if you were unfortunate enough to miss the last bus home.

The dance hall was the first thing to be seen on entering Thornley, a low, modern construction of mostly brick, left of the main thoroughfare. It was complemented by a working men's club opposite. On Saturday night, the club became the first port of call for many, before, fortified by liquid courage, they crossed the road to the dance. The main street wound upwards to a residential area at the top. I thought it was faintly reminiscent of the main street that ran through Houghton at that time. It consisted mostly of shops, but there was a cinema about half way up on the left.

The Thornley dance had a nice atmosphere. The dance floor occupied the ground floor – I don't recall an upstairs – while about a third of the space was given over to a refreshment area. When you tired of dancing, you could take a break, sit at a table, and enjoy a refreshing lemonade or orange squash. After taking in the scene and threading our way through the crowd

One of Thornley's pubs – The Halfway House.

on the margin of the floor, Albert and I took seats at one of the tables. In no time at all, we got into conversation with a couple of local girls who were sitting out a foxtrot. Once a degree of familiarity had been established, they allowed us to buy them a fruit squash. They were likeable, modest girls who, so they told us, had been friends since childhood. We seemed to pair off naturally. I took to one of them, Margaret by name, right off, and it was plain that her friend, a petite blonde, was making an impression on Albert, and he on her. I was amazed how, in such a relaxed atmosphere, and in the absence of the need to create an impression, I could find so much to talk about. Quite soon, I was able to put the humiliation I had felt after the Easington debacle behind me.

At the end of the night, when the orchestra was packing up and everybody was making for the exits, Albert and I walked the two girls up the main street to where they lived, with an eye on our watches, so as not to miss the last bus back to Murton. We met the following Saturday by arrangement, and soon the two of us were travelling through to Thornley in mid week. Sometimes the four of us went to the pictures, but mainly we went for walks, regularly strolling over to nearby Wheatley Hill and back, a round trip of about a mile and a half. It reminded me of the walk between Murton and the Waterworks and was about the same distance.

Alas, our association with the two Thornley girls didn't last long; a few weeks at most. I think it was the remoteness of the place that put paid to it. Albert and I had always to keep in mind not to miss the last bus back to Murton, and there was always the apprehension that, sooner or later, we almost certainly would. The dance scene moved from Thornley to somewhere else; and, once again, Saturday night found me with the other half of Murton at the second house at the Empire.

Chapter Eight
Hi-De-Hi

Holidays with pay was a catch-phrase of the post-war years, when, for one or possibly two weeks every summer, growing numbers of mineworkers and their families took a leave of absence from work and home to seek sun and recreation in distant parts. The practice of going by air to destinations abroad in quest of guaranteed sunshine took off in the 1960s. Before then, Filey on the North Yorkshire coast was the favourite holiday destination for many. The former fishing village became a Mecca for holidaymakers after Billy Butlin, a man I greatly admired, opened his holiday camp there in the first year after the war, work on the camp having been curtailed following the outbreak of hostilities. For a while, Butlins, Filey became the summer playground of the North Eastern mineworker and his family.

Filey wasn't the only Butlins camp, of course, but it was conveniently close to home, being only a short distance beyond the Yorkshire moors. Some holidaymakers later ventured further afield, to the camps at Skegness, Ayr and elsewhere; but it's safe to say that, as in my case, for most Murton campers, Filey will have been their first experience of a Butlins holiday.

The holidays were affordable and were all inclusive. Accommodation was in quaint but serviceable chalets, which were constructed in neat, colourful rows, separated by spacious lawns and ornamented by flower beds. Meals were taken at one of several dining halls, and all entertainment was free. Only drinks from the numerous on site bars had to be paid for. People saved all year round to pay for the holiday. Family men, accompanied by their wives and children, and parties of friends, mostly teens and twenties, many of the younger ones holidaying for the first time away from parental influence, joined the holiday coaches for the road south over the moors. Or else they travelled by rail, disembarking at Butlins own railway station, the culmination of a branch line specially created to serve the camp. Few in those days owned a car. Butlins holiday camp at Filey once held a place in the Guinness Book of Records as the biggest holiday camp in the world. I know of some who were put off by its size, and who expressed a preference for smaller camps such as Ayr.

The indoor and outdoor swimming pools at Butlins holiday camp, Filey.

Filey was laid out roughly in the form of a grid, the focal point being the swimming and diving pool, the scene of many regattas, where swimmers were pitted in competition with one another for the amusement of their fellow campers. The Filey camp was noted for its many brick buildings, and for being designed on more than one level, with, here and there, flights of steps ascending to a higher plane. Flowering shrubs and bushes grew in profusion by the sides of the steps and brightened the land bordering the roads through the camp.

Campers were organized into houses, which took their names from the names given to the four dining halls, Gloucester, Windsor, Kent and York. On my first Filey holiday, taken with Mam and Dad and my younger brothers shortly before I began work, we were seated in the Gloucester dining room, so Gloucester became our house. The names were not merely convenient labels; they were insignia, and the rallying cry of much inter-house rivalry, which was a staple ingredient of holiday camp entertainment, at least in the early days.

The Redcoats were the cheerleaders and motivators. Redcoats were assigned to a house, and they would organize committees made up of campers, and plan contests against other houses, which took place in or around the swimming pool or on the sports field. Dad was appointed to the house committee on one Butlins holiday, chosen, I suspect, because the Redcoat in charge, Watty Graham, came from Murton.

To be a Redcoat you had to be a good mixer. If you passed one of them in the camp, you could expect to be hailed with the Butlins catch-phrase, "Hi-De-Hi!" a greeting said to have been borrowed from a Cab Calloway film. Or you could take the initiative in greeting them, and be acknowledged by the cheery rejoinder "Ho-De-Ho!" Redcoats stood out from the crowd in their bright red blazers and cream slacks, or pleated

Murton Campers at Butlins, Ayr with Murton redcoat Watty Graham around 1960.

skirts in the case of the women, although both men and women sometimes wore shorts. Their blazer displayed the enamel Butlins badge, which was also given to every camper, and the men usually sported the striped Butlins tie

Throughout the day, when not supervising sporting contests, the Redcoats would be kept busy overseeing numerous events that took place indoors. If they weren't co-ordinating the fancy dress parade, they might be judging the entrants in such disparate categories as bonny babies or glamorous grandmothers, the latter event supposedly having been inspired by the celebrated Hollywood grandmother, Marlene Dietrich. On certain days, if the weather was kind, crowds would converge on the swimming pool, where the clamour of partisan voices, much laughter, and a considerable displacement of water betokened the light hearted, if determined, business of poolside, inter-house rivalry. Because of this organizational aspect, some superior persons who had never been to a Butlins camp would sometimes sneeringly refer to them as concentration camps. But, of course, participation in competitive events was purely voluntary. No one was obliged to become involved – I never did – and there was plenty to do, day and night, for those not drawn to inter-house competition.

The day began with a waking call from Radio Butlin, and a reminder that breakfast would be served in the dining hall shortly. Most would already be up and dressed by then, and perhaps enjoying an early morning coffee in one of the coffee bars. Meal times were an essential part of a Butlin holiday. There was a special atmosphere when you entered the dining hall and were greeted by the heavy drone of voices of innumerable campers, and the constant clatter of cutlery and crockery being moved about. The walk down the aisle to the accustomed table gave rise to friendly exchanges with fellow campers who, on the first day, were complete strangers, but who, after two or three mealtimes, had become familiar faces.

Having your meals served by polite, dining room staff was a pleasurable experience, especially, I imagine, for normally hard pressed wives and mothers who, for fifty one days in the year, fulfilled that function themselves, after having first cooked the meals. The food was plain, nothing fancy, but wholesome and appetizing. The waiters and waitresses were invariably pleasant, even if they always seemed to be rushed off their feet. When one of them dropped a plate, the whole building erupted into cheers as it hit the floor. There was never a mealtime when it didn't happen, which led me to wonder if they didn't drop plates on purpose. Had they been instructed to sacrifice the odd plate to enliven the place and contribute to the esprit de corps, the sense of sharing in the fun of a Butlins holiday?

It was at breakfast that the programme of events would be scrutinized and discussed, and the day's activities planned. As there was so much entertainment of a competitive sort, both to see, and, possibly, to take part in, a certain amount of selectivity became necessary, and events which might have been enjoyed had sometimes to be given a miss when they clashed with those holding greater appeal.

Those of a lazy, perhaps contemplative, nature were not disregarded. One of the bars had an extended lounge overlooking the pool. It could be busy at night, but not so much during the day. Here you could relax in the comfort of one of the armchairs, read a

The dining room at Butlins, Filey.

A Murton family sitting down for a meal at Butlins, Ayr in 1960.

newspaper, perhaps, or take your time over a drink. Alternatively, if you were not drawn to competitive events but were energetic, you might want to try navigating your way around the camp in one of the two-seater pedal vehicles that, once you got the momentum going, could reach a fair speed, but which were less governable than they appeared. To claim one, all you had to do was deposit your chalet key with the person

EDMUND DRIVE, BUTLIN'S LUXURY HOLIDAY CAMP, FILEY.

A postcard of Butlins 'Luxury' holiday camp at Filey.

in charge. This would be returned to you once you had finished with the conveyance and handed it over.

The pleasant, if contrived, surroundings, and the smooth road surfaces, made for an enjoyable stroll around the camp. You could stop off at one or other of the gift shops, or take advantage of the postal service, which enabled you to buy stamps and postcard views of the camp to send to friends and relatives at home.

The camp photographer would be on hand each and every day, snapping campers as they passed by; sometimes getting them to pose by one of the fountains on the margin of the swimming pool. Or, at their own request, he would snap them as they posed with an obliging Redcoat who happened to be on hand. One day every week, he circled the dining hall, taking pictures of families and friends, while they paused in what they were doing to pose for him. Later in the week, possibly the next day, the photographs would be displayed in the window of the photographic shop for those who wished to buy.

As was inevitable during the miners' fortnight, wherever you went in the camp, you were bound to meet those you knew. I loved running into Murton folk. But not everyone felt that way, and there were those who avoided Filey during the first week of the holidays precisely for that reason.

In the evening, the wide variety of professional entertainment to be found in the theatres and bars ensured that no preference was neglected. Children's shows, conducted by a resident "Uncle", usually with the assistance of a Recoat or two, began early, before the start of the adult shows. At the end of the week, The Redcoats put on their own show, to general acclaim. A highly professional performance could be expected, for, as is well known, many now famous celebrities kick started their careers in show business working as Butlins Redcoats.

A comic duo known as Mick and Montmorency were doing a season at Filey during my first stay at the camp. The act was a great favourite of people of my age. Sitting in the next row to me in the audience were George and Jimmy Rutherford, whom I knew from school and from playing on the same football team. The contrasting appearance of the two comics formed the basis of their knockabout routine. One was a hulking, overbearing type; the other, the object of his partner's rough treatment, was a puny, diminutive chap with blonde curly hair and a high pitched voice. After going solo and changing his name to Charley Drake, he became a household name, the comic star of at least one popular British film, and the recording star of that unforgettable classic, My Boomerang Won't Come Back.

For those of a different disposition, there were quiet retreats where it was possible to recline in comfort while gratifying a partiality for conversation, alcohol, and, in common with many pleasure seekers then, whatever form of relaxation they hankered after, tobacco.

On my first night, I fell in with a detachment of Murton youths who were bound for one of the theatres, where live wrestling was taking place. It was an extremely raucous atmosphere, and most of the noise was emanating from the Murton contingent, who appeared to have appropriated most of the seats near the front, and who, in a juvenile sort of way, seemed intent on making their presence known. During the bouts, they would leap up and down, gesticulating wildly while shouting words of encouragement to one or other of the contestants. The referee came in for some good natured booing if the decision he gave was an unpopular one. It was all harmless fun, appreciated, I'm sure, by the performers, who, spurred on by the vocal support, were playing to the gallery. Sidney Mundin, soon to become better known to me as a marra in the Five Quarter South Drifts, was sitting on the end seat in the front row. Every so often, Sidney would start from his seat and make a bolt for the ringside, where he would yell demonically "Shazam!" at the grapplers on the canvass, the significance of which bizarre behaviour being known only to himself.

Many people went to Filey with not much more than one thing in mind, that of taking part in the ballroom dancing, which was staged nightly in the Viennese ballroom, and in the end of week ballroom competition. Lessons in dancing were given during the day by professional instructors. But the folk who flocked to the Viennese ballroom were not interested beginners but enthusiasts who, throughout the course of the year, were accustomed to going dancing several times a week. Dancing was their passion, and they were every one of them accomplished performers. The women came resplendent in magnificent ball gowns of various colours and hues, set off with sequins and acres of lace; while the men were handsomely garbed in well cut dark suits and bow ties.

The first dance festival to be held at Filey took place the year of my first Butlin holiday. Nothing else in the camp could quite compare with the spectacle of the Viennese ballroom. Ivy Benson and her all-girl band was the resident band that year. It was a very famous band at the time, sufficiently famous to become the subject of a recent television documentary tribute. I took a shine to the blonde drummer, and was thrilled when Ivy Benson did me the favour of signing my autograph book.

Filey was a popular destination for Durham families during miners' fortnight.

I had bought the book at a time when I was in regular attendance at Roker Park on alternate Saturday afternoons. Beyond the first two pages, the book remained blank. The few autographs I managed to obtain belonged to Sunderland footballers, Tommy Wright and Johnny Mapson figuring prominently among them. Interest in autograph hunting eventually evaporated, and the book was put to one side. I took it with me to Butlins because you never knew what famous personalities you might meet there. I regretted not having asked Charley Drake for his autograph, but I wasn't to know he would become famous.

One day, I spotted a body of men in smart, executive suits at the end of a row of chalets. They were pointing this way and that, engrossed in earnest deliberation; it seemed obvious that they were discussing plans of some sort. I did a double take when I spied Billy Butlin among their number. Sprinting the two

Above: Murton children at Filey in 1963.

Charlie Drake – a popular entertainer in the 1950s and '60s.

Billy Butlin signing autographs.

hundred yards or so to my chalet, I grabbed my autograph book and a pen from a drawer in the chest of drawers and hared off back to where I had left them, hoping all the while that they hadn't concluded their business and moved on. But they were still in the same place, still engrossed in discussion. For a few moments I hung around on the periphery, before a tall, distinguished looking man noticed me standing at his side, autograph book in hand. Indicating his boss, he said, "Go on, ask him." Encouraged by this, I stepped forward to come face to face with Billy Butlin. In my most respectful voice, I asked him for his autograph. "Sure," he beamed good-naturedly, reaching for the book, before kindly appending his signature. I politely thanked him, before dashing off to find my friends and show them my trophy. Billy Butlin was never going to refuse his autograph to a young boy holidaying at one of his own camps. But I sensed that he was the sort of man who would have co-operated anyway.

A week was never quite enough at Butlins. Once the weekend was out of the way, the days just seemed to fly by. In no time at all, the holiday had come to an end, and campers would be loading their cases onto the coaches for the homeward journey over the moors. Schoolchildren still had several weeks of freedom before returning to school. For adults, it would be a quick return, either to the daily domestic routine, or to the dull, repetitive cycle of first, back, nights and tub loadin'.

The roller skating rink at Butlins, Ayr in 1960.

Chapter Nine
Television and other Marvels

Today, it is hard to imagine a living room without a television. But there was a time when the radio, or wireless as it was called then, retained a place in the home currently occupied by the television set.

Many a leisurely hour was whiled away in the company of radio personalities such as Gracie Fields, whose broadcast once famously caused the House of Commons to break up early so that honourable members would not have to miss it; and Tommy Handley, the star of ITMA (It's That Man Again), a show that incorporated comic sketches and gave rise to numerous catch-phrases. Whereas today the news is brought graphically to the attention of the public as and wherever it is taking place, previously people learned of news events over the air waves. The wireless was never more relevant than during the war, and not only for imparting news. Wartime listeners were cheered in equal measure by Winston Churchill's rousing jingoistic speeches and by the patriotic sentiments in the songs of Vera Lynn, Anne Shelton and Gracie Fields. Not a few long-running radio shows were carried over from wartime. Music While You Work and Workers' Playtime were two, while Two-Way Family favourites began as the war was ending.

Older devotees of Coronation Street will recall the legendary, sharp-tongued battleaxe, Ena Sharples, memorably brought to life by the actress, Violet Carson. Long before her debut in Coronation Street, Miss Carson appeared in a radio show which was broadcast from the Murton pit canteen. The show was the hugely successful Have a Go, compered by Wilfred Pickles, a down to earth Yorkshireman, actor, news reader and quiz show host. Pickles toured the country with his show, in which he was assisted by his wife Mabel (at the table), and by Barney Colehan, the show's producer, who was urged to "Give him the money, Barney" whenever someone successfully answered the few simple questions which entitled him to claim the money prize. Violet Carson was the show's pianist. Local audiences at the start of each show were greeted with Pickles' famous catchword, "How do, how are yer?" Contestants were required, as a preliminary, to answer such personal questions as "Are yer courtin'?" and "Have you ever had an embarrassing moment?" In retrospect, it all seems very unsophisticated, and it might well be thought that participation in the show should qualify as an embarrassing moment.

The latest and best radio and record player combined.

If Have a Go foreshadowed the television quiz shows of today, then it was PC 49 and Dixon of Dock Green who were the precursors of the police procedural dramas such as Z Cars, The Bill and Frost. But neither the plodding PC Archibald Barclay nor the avuncular George Dixon quite achieved the distinction of the Secret Service operator,

Dick Barton. Dick Barton, Special Agent was a serial drama of fifteen minute episodes. Each episode commenced and concluded with a frenetic, breakneck commentary spoken over the theme tune with the inspired choice of name, The Devil's Gallop. Noel Johnson played the Secret Service agent on radio. At the height of the show's popularity, three films were made featuring Don Stannard as Dick Barton. A runaway success, the film series ended in 1949 with the premature death, at thirty-three, of Stannard; but the radio series continued into the fifties. When it ended with the main character being killed off, it gave rise to a public outcry. However, unlike Sherlock Holmes and one of the principal characters in Dallas, Barton made no post mortem appearances. Instead, the Dick Barton radio slot was filled by a new, rural drama called The Archers, which eventually became the longest-running radio serial ever.

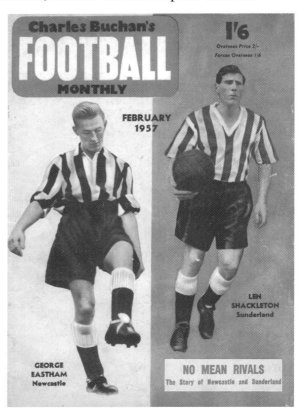

A copy of Charlie Buchan's Football Monthly with Len Shackleton on the front cover.

In the 1954 World Cup Final, West Germany unexpectedly defeated Hungary, the greatest national side of the mid 1950s, and arguably the greatest side never to have won the competition. It was doubly unexpected, because when the sides met in an earlier round of the competition, Hungary put seven goals past the Germans. Soon after, England played the new world champions at Wembley, when the match was televised. The medium was in its nascent stage and had yet to take off in this country. Mr and Mrs Salkeld, who were neighbours of ours, owned a new television set. Mr Salkeld invited Dad and me to their house to watch the match. Also present, were a next door neighbour and the couple's sons, Jack, who was a little older than me, and George, who was slightly younger. In an atmosphere of wonder and excitement, we watched England beat the Germans 3-1, and were pleased to note that Sunderland's Len Shackleton scored one of the goals. It was the first time I had ever seen television.

Presently, Dad bought a set, which took pride of place in the corner of our living room. Soon, it seemed almost everybody in Murton was displaying the distinctive H shaped aerial above the roof of the house. Television sets in those early days were

either 12 inch or 14 inch, and the picture was, of course, black and white. Within a year, anyone keen to keep abreast of television technology would be in possession of the latest set, with what seemed at the time the colossal 17 inch screen. Television sets could hardly get bigger, I thought, when I first saw the 17 inch screen in the living room of Albert Swan's house.

To begin with, programme planners were faced with the problem of finding sufficient material to fill the available slots, and much early television consisted of American imports, such as the Amos and Andy Show and the Burns and Allen Show. The former was an ethnic comedy with an all-black cast. Although funny, it wasn't as funny as the Burns and Allen Show. George Burns and Gracie Allen were already famous as a husband and wife comedy act. In addition to their radio work, they had worked with Bing Crosby and W.C.

An early television.

Fields, among other big names, in Hollywood films of the 1930s and 1940s, and were stars in their own right.

The format of the Burns and Allen show was uncomplicated and unvarying. A series of callers would arrive at the house when George was out, to be entertained by the scatterbrained Gracie. In everything she said, Gracie observed a total disregard for logic, and nothing she said ever had any relevance to the matter in hand. Completely bewildered, the visitor beat a hasty retreat, leaving behind his hat, which became the latest addition to Gracie's collection of men's hats that had been forgotten in the urge to get away. One caller, frustrated beyond endurance, his brain mashed to pulp by Gracie's tortuous flights of unreason, passed George on his way out, and, handing him his card, uttered the unforgettable line: "I'm a lawyer. If you ever do what you should do, I'll defend you free of charge."

The Burns and Allen Show, like the Amos and Andy Show, enjoyed enormous success, in part, at least, due to a lack of competition. But these early forays into television comedy were soon superseded by a vogue in series entertainment unique in British television, the like of which has not been seen since. Throughout much of the decade, TV screens were monopolized by a seemingly unending series of American, made-for-television films of a genre that had long been a staple of Hollywood, namely, the Western. A list of television programmes from the era would be likely to include Cheyenne, Bronco, Tenderfoot, Wyatt Earp, Bonanza, Waggon Train, Laramie, to give merely a token and flavour of the trend, for the list is by no means exhaustive. Westerns were screened several times nightly, the film of one series being followed by that of another. Some films had an itinerant bent and typically narrated the adventures of a lonesome western hero as he pursued his nomadic way of life. Such was the pattern for Tenderfoot, Bronco and Cheyenne. The theme song of the last mentioned

Advertising televisions in the run up to the 1955 Cup Final.

included the lyric, "Cheyenne, where will you be camping tonight?" Waggon Train, and the cattle drive epic, Rawhide, each chronicled the fortunes of an itinerant group of people as distinct from those of an individual.

Other series of the genre were more sedentary, some being situated in western towns – Gunsmoke, Laramie, Wyatt Earp – or on a ranch – Bonanza, and, at a later date, The Big Valley. Many of these western series featured established Hollywood actors in the lead roles. But they also gave rise to new stars. The giant sized Clint Walker made the transition from the small screen to become a star of the big screen. Ty Hardin, the eponymous hero of Bronco, also carved a niche for himself in feature films, until he adopted extremist views and became the leader of a neo-Fascist political party. Eric Fleming, who played the trail boss, Gil Favor in Rawhide, was set for a glittering Hollywood career before he drowned in a river in South America while on a film location shoot. But it is doubtful if Eric Fleming would ever have achieved the star magnitude of the actor who played the supporting role in the Rawhide series, Clint Eastwood.

The television western series had all but expired by the onset of the 1960s, when television programmers found other ways of filling the TV screens. With hindsight, it seems difficult to credit that fifties viewers, women included, should have been engrossed in an interminable cycle of escapades involving western heroes. However, it should be recalled that television then was still in its infancy, and that there wasn't too much else to watch. Also, that every one of these essentially male-orientated series featured rugged young men in leading roles, even when the main role was taken by an established, middle-aged actor. The rancher in Bonanza, played by Lorne Greene, had three young sons. Ward Bond, the wagon master in Waggon Train, was supported by Robert Horton, who played the young scout. Throughout the entire period, posters of Horton, Michael Landon, Ty Hardin, Clint Walker and other western pin ups adorned the walls of many a teenage girl's bedroom.

It was evident that the new medium, which brought drama directly into the home, posed a threat to the film industry, and put the continued existence of cinemas in jeopardy. In 1953, a revolution of sorts occurred in the film industry, which was, however, not so much a response to the challenge laid down by television, but rather a development in the process of film making. Pictures in the 3D (three-dimensional) process were capturing everyone's imagination. At the same time, Twentieth Century Fox introduced its own cinematic innovation, Cinemascope.

The first 3D picture seen in Murton was the gimmicky, one-reeler, A Day in the Country, which the Empire screened to packed houses. The picture gave rise to much hilarity, as members of the audience could be seen averting the head to avoid various farmyard objects, like a pitchfork or the rear end of a cow, which appeared to be projected straight at them from the screen. Subsequently, a few feature length pictures were made in this process before interest in it waned.

The first feature film made in Cinemascope was the biblical epic, The Robe, starring Richard Burton and Jean Simmons. It was exhibited in Sunderland at the Regal, where I saw it one Saturday afternoon. The reaction was electric. Hitherto, cinema screens had been squarish. As the soundtrack music was heard to introduce the opening scene, a slave market in ancient Rome, the curtains went back. And back. And back. The screen appeared to occupy the entire back wall of the cinema.

The visual effects of the picture were accompanied by stereophonic sound, which came from all parts of the auditorium, completely surrounding the audience. When shown on television, the film is certainly watchable, but no sense is conveyed of the impact it made on the wide screen. In a scene following the arrest of Jesus, a lone, forlorn figure is apprehended in a deserted side street. In a dramatic display of conscience searching, he reveals himself to be Judas. At the sound of the word, an ear-splitting peal of thunder resounded from the rear of the auditorium, and I

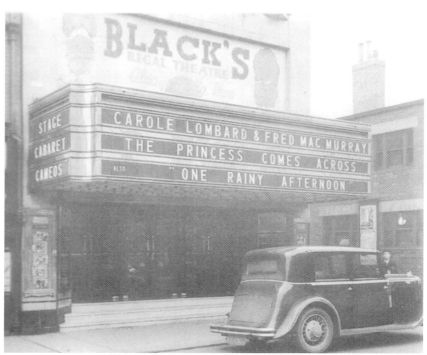

Black's Regal Cinema in Sunderland in the 1940s.

don't mind admitting that it sent a shiver coursing down my spine.

The success of The Robe led to other Cinemscope productions, and it wasn't long before cinemas everywhere were equipped to show pictures in the new process. Paramount Pictures came up with something called VistaVision, which, while there were technical differences of which audiences may or may not have been aware, was hardly dissimilar to Cinemascope. Kiddo thought 3D was the future. I was more impressed with Cinemascope. I thought 3D had nothing more than novelty appeal, and that picturegoers would soon tire of the need to wear special glasses every time they went to the cinema.

About the time these technological innovations in film were taking place, something of a revolution was occurring in the field of popular music. I suppose fifty's music is associated in most people's minds with the advent of rock 'n' roll; and, sadly, the music that preceded it seems to have been largely forgotten. It is sad to note that recording artists of the calibre of Frankie Laine, Guy Mitchell, Tennessee Ernie Ford and the Four Aces among many others are hardly ever mentioned today. Yet all were big names at the time.

Frankie Laine and Guy Mitchell both made appearances in trendy, musical films of the era. The Sunny Side of the Street, Those Redheads from Seattle, and Red Garters spring to mind. In addition to his powerful renditions of classic songs like Jezebel and Granada, Frankie Laine supplied the soundtrack voice for several notable films, mostly westerns, including Blowing Wild and Gunfight at the OK Corral, and for the TV series, Rawhide.

Tennessee Ernie Ford lent his distinctive rich voice to the theme song of the Robert Mitchum/Marilyn Monroe western, River of No Return, while the romantic weepie, Love is a Many Splendored Thing is chiefly remembered for the title song, which was recorded by the all-male singing group, the Four Aces and which featured on the soundtrack of the film.

Someone on the staff of the Murton Empire must have been a Guy Mitchell fan, for whenever you went there, one or more of his recordings could usually be heard prior to the start of the programme. The Mitch Miller orchestra that provided the orchestral backing for Guy Mitchell was as famous as the artist. The prominent use of French horns, combined with the rhythmic hand-clapping and mixed male and female voices of the backing choir lent a unique sound to such lively numbers as Truly Fair, Sparrow in the Tree Top, and She Wears Red Feathers.

Albert was always conversant with the latest developments in popular music. When I called at his house one day, he was eager to have me listen to something by the new recording sensation, Slim Whitman, whom I had not heard of. He had just released his version of Rose Marie, which, as Albert said, he was able to put over in a uniquely different way. Rose Marie was a song from an operetta of the same name, and was always voiced by a classically-trained tenor or baritone. Slim Whitman was essentially a country singer. He not so much sang the song as yodelled it. Yet when I heard his version I was bowled over by it. It seemed incredible that anyone could yodel his way through operetta. Yet Rose Marie and the Indian Love Call from the same show were huge hits for the singer, whose inimitable rendition of a song was subsequently imparted to Danny Boy, Beautiful Dreamer and other unlikely

A popular recording artist and the soundtrack voice on many films.

The top male recording group of the 1950s.

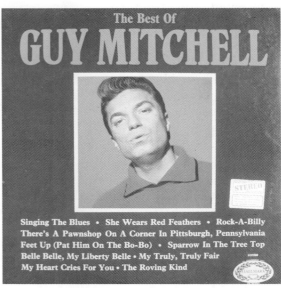

Guy Mitchell recorded many top hits with the Mitch Miller Orchestra.

ballads, which, when given the Slim Whitman treatment, also became massive hits.

Records then were the 10 inch vinyl kind, 12 inch in the case of operatic records, and numbered only two tunes, one on each side of the record. As with most of the record-buying public, I went to the Gordon Eades music shop in Sunderland to buy records. The shop was located in a side street off Fawcett Street. Gordon Eades sold mostly pianos, but in a department at the rear of the shop, which was always busiest, it was possible to buy any of the latest recordings. Indeed, the shop stocked records of every musical genre. The young assistant, a tall, unruffled woman of slim build, was always on hand to deal with requests. Your Cheatin' Heart, the Roving Kind, Wheel of Fortune, these could be promptly dealt with. Requests for Celeste Aida, One Fine Day or the Nuns' Chorus

Slim Whitman brought a country flavour to songs like Rose Marie and Danny Boy.

could take a little longer. But I never knew her to admit defeat. No matter what your musical preference, Gordon Eades would stock it. You could approach the counter and ask, say, "Do you have the Intermezzo from Cavaleria Rusticana by the Dresden State Opera Orchestra – must be the Dresden State?" The assistant would furrow her brow, murmur, "Let me see now," before running her finger along the serried rows of record covers, eventually coming to rest on one. "Yes, here we are." That same day, you would be listening to it on your wind-up gramophone. I never had to order anything from Gordon Eades. All my requests – and I was buying opera at the time – were dealt with there and then.

Albert had a knack for spotting upcoming talent. One day, he begged me to come and listen to his latest acquisition, a recording by someone with a name that seemed to me so unusual I had to ask Albert to repeat it. According to Albert, he had a voice that ranged over I don't know how many octaves. I listened with interest to the recording, although I was not as captivated by it as Albert was. The song was Heartbreak Hotel. In no time at all, the singer, Elvis Presley, had become a global sensation. About the same time, Bill Haley and the Comets made a triumphant debut with the hit song, and film of the same name, Rock Around the Clock. Rock 'n' Roll had arrived.

An advert for Gordon Eades, Fawcett Street, Sunderland, recommending HMV (His Master's Voice) products.

Not all artists emerging at the time were inflexibly wedded to the new musical craze, but included the likes of Paul Anka, Neil Sedaka, Connie Francis, the Everly Brothers, Buddy Holly, Brenda Lee – I might perhaps be forgiven the catalogue, which is incomplete and representative only. Some of these artists became perennial favourites. After that, it was only a few short years before the next seismic shift in musical taste transpired, when the focus switched to England and Liverpool.

Chapter Ten
Leaving Home

For more than a year, Albert and I worked together as a team at the West Pit shaft bottom. The job was hardly different from the work I had been doing in the South Drifts and, before then, at bank. Tubs were projected from the cage empty and quickly coupled together and dregged. At the appropriate moment, they were shifted to a place between two ventilation doors, having room for only eight tubs, when they were again dregged. Once the door nearest the shaft had been shut tight, the chummins were lowered down a gradient, before being connected up to the main set. When the set was complete, it was hauled inbye by means of the main and tail.

Only one of the ventilation doors could be left open at any one time. If both doors remained open, as only infrequently happened when a tub came off the way in the doorway, then the down current of air clashed with the up current and a dust storm ensued, enveloping everyone in the vicinity in blinding dust. The situation could be righted only when the tub was lifted back on the way and the door closed. It was a two-man job, one man handling the tubs as they left the cage, and the other labouring between and beyond the ventilation doors. To ward off any sense of tedium, Albert and I exchanged routines every hour.

The foreman, Jossy Ord, was a busy man, who was always on the telephone. He had the responsibility for ensuring that the set got off without mishap or delay, so the men inbye and at the coal face would not be idle. The team included the two onsetters, Davy Bunker and Joe Neasham, Davy harsh of voice but mild of manner, Joe, unflappable, forever chewing tobacco. These three men were considerably older than the rest of the workforce.

Jossy was short and stout and red-faced. It sometimes happened that one of us, usually me, allowed the chummins to descend the gradient too fast, so that one or more came off the way when they collided with those at the bottom and had to be lifted back on. At the sound of crashing tubs, Jossy would come out of his cabin and gesture helplessly; or, if it was happening too often, go into a tirade. But Jossy's bark was worse than his bite. We all knew he could never be angry with anyone for long. Everybody liked Jossy.

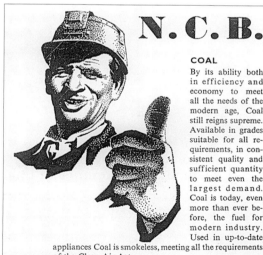
An advert for the National Coal Board from the 1950s.

Completing the crew and working in proximity to Albert and myself, were Billy Parker and Billy Wylde, both strong, powerfully built lads. Being all about the same age, we enjoyed a certain rapport. At the end of the night shift, about 11.00 p.m., we were never in any hurry to go home, but spent ages dawdling in the pit baths, and were there long after the older men had left for home. Billy Wylde was perhaps the most level-headed amongst us, and he would be the first to get dressed and depart. Some evenings, the four of us, together with Joe Neasham, who had a car, would go for a drive. Once we took it into our heads to go for a swim, only we motored to Redcar, where we had a great time in the indoor swimming pool on the sea front.

We once walked to Hawthorn, not with any particular object in mind. It was a leisurely, purposeless walking for walking's sake, which sometimes took us to destinations which had not been of anyone's choosing at the outset of the walk.

Hawthorn is a picturesque village off the Sunderland to Stockton road, perhaps a mile and a half south-east of Murton as the crow flies, twice that if journeying by road. The focal point of the village is the parish church, where, adjacent to it, there was a fine village hall.

When we arrived, a dance was in progress in celebration of someone's birthday. One of our number, probably Billy Parker, knew some of the people present. It seems more likely to have been he, for, following his marriage, Billy went to live in the village. Thanks to Billy, our little group was able to gate crash the party. Having said that, the Hawthorn people were friendly enough, and, despite our outsider status, we were not made to feel unwelcome.

Hawthorn Village.

There are certain events in the course of a life, and I think this is true of everyone, that are of no great moment, but, for one reason or another, are held dear and savoured long after in recall. Am I being too philosophical? Well, among my memories, such an event was the night of the youth dance

Hawthorn Parish Church.

in Hawthorn. It was an old time dance. All the time-honoured favourites – the Boston Two Step, the Eva Three Step, the Dashing White Sergeant, the Lancers – that I had become familiar with in merry evenings passed away in St. Joseph's church hall and had since forgotten, were danced with gleeful exuberance by the company of seventeen and eighteen year olds, whose exclamations of joy reverberated around the hall. It didn't take long for me to become reacquainted with the old dances; after that, you couldn't have dragged me off the floor. I never discovered whose birthday it was; but I hope the occasion gave to that person as much pleasure as it gave to me.

Later, when the party broke up and folks drifted away, we got the bus home; or rather two buses, one to the Waterworks and one from there across to Murton. It was a weird state of affairs, a combined result of geographical location and the operations of multiple bus companies, that if you wanted to go to or from Hawthorn and you didn't want to walk, then you had to take two buses. At any other time, we would have walked the distance, no matter how late the hour, but we were fairly worn out by our exertions on the dance floor, me most of all.

Teens and twenties parties might have been more common then than they are today, although most were held in the home rather than in a public place. The church huts in Murton bore some comparison with the village hall in Hawthorn. The only time I was in the church huts was when I was a guest at a party

Before cars became more common, most people got around by bus. Here is the Northern Bus No 152 alongside the Independent Methodist Church at the top of the Terrace.

to celebrate Maurice Lilley's birthday. Mrs Lilley and my mother were great friends. Our two families had been neighbours in Glenhurst Terrace, which was my place of birth. When I was about two, we moved to Church Lane, opposite the entrance to St. Joseph's school yard, but Mam and Dad remained always on friendly terms with Mr and Mrs Lilley. Maurice was five years older than me, and as the other guests at the party were boys and girls in Maurice's age group, I felt a bit out of place. But it was like Mrs Lilley to insist that I be invited.

The last two years of school marked a season of party-going; they were mainly held by girls, when everyone in the class was invited. Gifts were taken, party games indulged in and much food was consumed. Betty and Mary White were both, at one time or another, in my class at school, and they always gave great parties. My mother had been a bridesmaid at their mother's wedding, the two of them having been friends from schooldays. The family lived in a big house between St Joseph's school and the Northern bus depot, and parties took place at the house at least twice a year.

As youngsters entered their late teens and early twenties, parties became more sophisticated. Alcoholic drinks, as well as the non alcoholic kind, were usually available. Nothing need be said about the latter; the former, it should be noted, were indulged in always in moderation. There was much animated debate of a more or less adult bent. Television being at an incipient stage, programmes of topical interest were much discussed, and the idiosyncracies of broadcasters like Peter Noble and Malcolm Muggeridge widely mimicked. There was always a piano, and always someone to play it. Pick any five girls at random, and one, at least, would be able to play the piano. If the living

Pianists were always in demand at parties.

room was big enough, the furniture might be moved back; then the space between would become a dance floor, if a somewhat cramped one. It was easy to get someone to warble the notes of a favourite song. Polite comments, that were not always strictly accurate, greeted every effort. "Doesn't he have a nice voice?" was the fulsome judgement once passed on my discordant baritone by a well-meaning girl older than me, after I had completed the demolition of the well-loved classic, Just a Song at Twilight.

Murton Colliery Band around 1970.

Apart from the piano, and discounting members of the Murton Colliery band and the Penman family band, musicians were otherwise fairly scarce. Unless, that is, you included in their number virtuosos on the mouth organ. There were any number of good mouth organists in Murton – Arthur Hunter, Jack Cooke, Ernie Ridley, Ernie Chant, Barney Adamson and, let no one accuse me of false modesty, myself. There were probably others that I never heard of. The instrument is known as a harp by some, by others as a harmonica; but Larry Adler, the best known practitioner, who often performed as a soloist with full symphony orchestras, always insisted that it was a mouth organ.

My mother bought me a mouth organ called London Pride. I subsequently occupied much of my spare time patiently practising, until I had mastered a few tunes. After that, I bought myself a Hohner, the Stradivarius of mouth organs, and after building up a repertoire of well known tunes, eventually discovered that I was able to vamp. You couldn't consider yourself an exponent of the mouth organ until you could vamp. To do this, you used your tongue, stopping and unstopping the spaces to provide a rhythmic backing to the notes produced by the passage of air through the reeds. Vamping can be described; it cannot be taught. It is an instinctive technique. But once you are able to find your way around the instrument, vamping should come naturally, so long as you are possessed of a sense of rhythm.

Arthur Hunter was the best player I knew, and I spent many hours taking note of his technique and trying to imitate it. At school, Arthur had been an ebullient extrovert who was always fun to be with. He was a born performer, who could sing, dance and tell jokes. Having served an apprenticeship at the pit and having worked there for some years, Arthur eventually left his job, and, after adopting the professional name of Alan McBride, became a professional entertainer. On one of his return visits to Murton, he was renewing old friendships over a drink in the concert room of the Demi Club when he was asked to oblige with a number. His choice of song was That's Amore, a romantic ditty made famous by Dean Martin. Arthur upped the tempo and sang it throughout in an Italian accent. It was an amazingly original interpretation of the song. The Demi Club was where you would often find me at weekends, although the High House and the Village Inn were also beneficiaries of my custom. I was drinking in several companies at this time. The liberality of Durham mining men, especially those of Irish descent, and especially when it comes to the buying of drinks, is well renowned; or if it isn't then it ought to be. Quite often, it almost seemed that a fight would ensue for the privilege of buying the first round.

"What'll ye have?"

"Aa'll get them."

"No. What are ye drinkin'?"

"Aa'll get them in, aa said."

"Put ye money away, Aa'm gettin' the drinks."

To give emphasis to the words, the money would sometimes be slapped down on the bar top. An outsider might be forgiven for feeling alarmed at these proceedings. Eventually, the barman would settle the dispute by sweeping someone's money off the bar top.

In time, I began going out with Dad, and his associates became my associates, even though they were already known to me and we were on good terms. They were all older than me. On a Sunday night, after church service, our company of five would become ensconced in the back room of the High House, Dad, myself, Mick Smith, who was

The Village Inn, sometimes known as the Murton Inn.

of the same generation as Dad, and Charley Hill and Joe Foley, who were both about ten years older that me. The back room was the music room, but it was not often that anyone was engaged to play the piano, and since most of the regulars thronged the bar, we always had the room to ourselves. The High House was a Scottish and Newcastle pub, and the landlord, Arthur Raymond, was known to keep a good pint. It was before the plague of slot machines, pool tables and television screens had descended upon public houses, and our little group whiled away the time in the profuse indulgence of appetites for good beer, tobacco, and lively conversation, interspersed with a great deal of laughter, as was unavoidable with Joe Foley in the company. If any one of us lacked anything, it certainly wasn't a sense of humour; and our hilarity burst out at intervals to rival that of the greater company in the bar. I was the only non smoker, but, by the end of the night, my secondary smoking must have accounted for quite a few cigarettes. The smoke stung my eyes, seeming to affect me more than it did the others. When the other four had taken a few puffs and about half a cigarette had gone, someone would pull a pack out and deal them across the table, like dealing cards.

The Sunday night ritual in the High House was shortened when St. Joseph's cashed in on the bingo craze, that had only then taken hold, to run a bingo in the church hall after Sunday evening services. However, it quickly became apparent that the church hall wasn't nearly big enough. Folks were flocking to the bingo, including many non-Catholics. This was before bingo came to be an ineradicable feature of the local club scene. Finally, the decision was taken to open the schools. Every Sunday, on the conclusion of the evening service, the men of the parish emptied the church of church benches, carrying them across the road to the school, before running the bingo, carrying them back into church when the bingo ended. The five of us being thus engaged, not a lot of time was left for socializing in the back room of the High House. Happily, the government obliged by extending the licensing hours from 10.00 p.m. to 10.30 p.m. to leave an extra half hour to closing time.

For some time now, I had been dissatisfied with my station in life, and had all but determined on a livelihood away from the pit. It was the impracticality of such a move that made me hesitate. There were few career opportunities for someone lacking qualifications. And even if I had gone into another occupation, within a very short time, weeks perhaps, months at most, I would assuredly have been called upon for National Service. Thus far, like all coal miners, I had been exempted from National Service. It was a combination of these and other factors – a boyish sense of adventure there certainly was – that caused me to give serious consideration to the Army as an alternative career.

My parents received the news in silence, once my mind was made up and I had informed them of my intent. I don't think either one was entirely happy for me to spend a lifetime working underground. Not all parents were content to see their sons committed to pit work if an optional way of life could be found. On the other hand, I knew they would be saddened to see me leave home. I think they concluded that I was old enough to make my own decisions regarding my future, and neither Mam nor Dad made any effort to dissuade me from the course of action I had decided upon. I got on a bus to Sunderland one day and paid a visit to the recruiting office, where I signed on for twenty-one years with a three year option.

I never gave the pit a backward glance when I finished my final shift. Once I had showered and dressed, I turned the key in my locker and left the pit baths for the last time. On the morning of my departure, I was up early. I had to get an early morning train to King's Cross and make my way from there to Blenheim Barracks in Aldershot. The previous night, Mam and Dad had maintained their silence and no goodbyes were said. It wasn't as if I was going off to war. It was the era of the Cold War. I would be engaging the Soviets, an enemy I was never to lay eyes on, my weapon, a typewriter. Still, I couldn't resist casting a backward glance as I closed the gate behind me. There was no one else about. The top half of the house was bathed in early morning sunlight, and, as I turned away, something stirred the curtain of my parents' bedroom.

A piece of Murton history – the old bridge over the railway line from Murton to Hetton.

70

Acknowledgements

I extend my warmest appreciation to the many people who have assisted in the production of this second volume of memoirs of Murton past.

For the loan of photographs and memorabilia, I am especially indebted to Gerard Short. Maureen Bartley and Tricia Pemberton were only too happy to oblige when handed a camera and despatched to numerous parts of the locality. George Maitland, Elaine Miller, David Salkeld and Keith Wren of the Murton Heritage Society willingly gave of their time in the selection and copying of photographs.

Several people, in addition, were kind enough to loan photographs, including my sister, Mary, who supplied most of the Butlin's pictures, and Derek Gillum, George Nairn, Trevor Williamson, Alan Brett, Phil Curtis and Sunderland Antiquarian Society.

Other illustrative material has added to the visual impact of the work. In this connection, Kevin Bartley's original art work merits special praise.

To the publisher Andrew Clark is owed my thanks for his commitment to the project; not forgetting the work involved in getting it into print.

A final word of thanks goes to my daughter, Colette, for the time and effort she spent in finalizing the typescript prior to its submission for consideration for publication.

P.J. McPartland

The multi-purpose Glebe Centre, home of many local activities including the Murton Heritage Society.

Also available from Summerhill Books

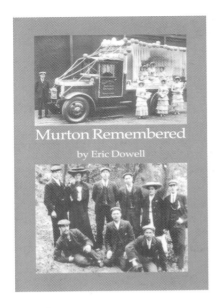

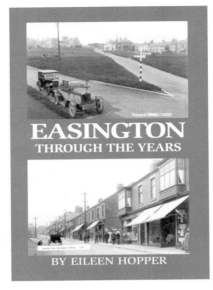

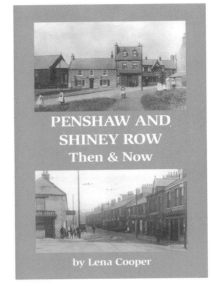

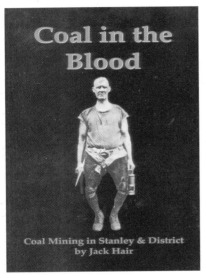

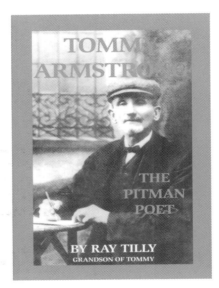

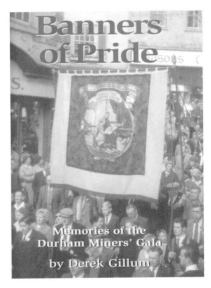

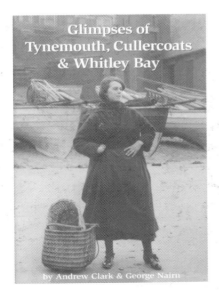

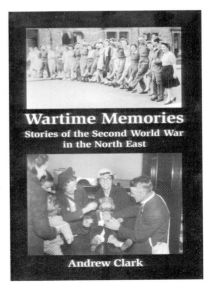

www.summerhillbooks.co.uk